Compensating the Sales Force

Compensating the Sales Force

David J. Cichelli

McGraw Hill

New York   Chicago   San Francisco   Lisbon   London
Madrid   Mexico City   Milan   New Delhi   San Juan
Seoul   Singapore   Sydney   Toronto

Copyright © 2004 by The McGraw-Hill Companies, Inc. All rights reserved. Printed in the United
States of America. Except as permitted under the United States Copyright Act of 1976, no part
of this publication may be reproduced or distributed in any form or by any means, or stored in
a data base or retrieval system, without the prior written permission of the publisher.

2 3 4 5 6 7 8 9 0   AGM/AGM   0 9 8 7 6 5 4 3

ISBN 0-07-141188-7

McGraw-Hill books are available at special quantity discounts to use as premiums and sales
promotions, or for use in corporate training programs. For more information, please write to
the Director of Special Sales, Professional Publishing, McGraw-Hill, Two Penn Plaza, New York,
NY 10121-2298. Or contact your local bookstore.

Library of Congress Cataloging-in-Publication Data

Cichelli, David J.
   Compensating the sales force: a practical guide to designing winning
sales compensation plans / by David J. Cichelli.
       p. cm.
Includes index.
   ISBN 0-07-141188-7
   1. Sales personnel—Salaries, etc.   2. Incentives in industry.   3.
Bonus system.   4. Compensation management.   I. Title.
   HF5439.7.C53 2004
   658.8'0068'3—dc21
                                                          2003008752

Dedication to
Mario and Genevieve Cichelli

Contents

Contents

Acknowledgments

Sales compensation affects tens of thousands, perhaps hundreds of thousands, of sales personnel on a worldwide basis who work with driven enthusiasm on behalf of their employers. Sales management professionals strive to create win-win opportunities for both sales personnel and their companies. It's been my pleasure to work with—and learn from—exceptional sales management leaders including Rick Justice at Cisco Systems, Karen Chang of Charles Schwab, and T. Michael Glenn at FedEx, plus hundreds of others who have helped me test and retest the sales compensation principles you will find in this book. I thank all of my clients who have contributed to building this emerging body of knowledge.

Special thanks must be given to WorldatWork (formerly the American Compensation Association), which has supported my work over the years, allowing me to create, modify, and improve sales compensation courses now taught to thousands of compensation and sales professionals. Without the opportunity to meet with so many compensation professionals in a classroom setting, the material in this book would not have met the test of time or reflect the challenges and suggestions of thousands of students. For this, I am most grateful to the continued support of Anne Ruddy, the Executive Director of WorldatWork. Additionally, WorldatWork has granted me permission to use select charts and concepts from these courses.

Additionally, I am grateful to the small cadre of professionals who have dedicated their careers to helping sales departments improve their sales compensation programs. The conceptual advances made by these individuals are intertwined into this book. They deserve special credit for their unique contributions to this subject: John Moynihan, Jerry Colletti, Stockton Colt, and Gary Schroeder.

My partners at The Alexander Group, Inc.—Gary Tubridy and Robert Conti—continue to provide their unflagging support and encouragement. Also, my fellow consultants never rest as they look for new sales effectiveness solutions to help clients adopt best-of-class sales growth solutions.

Although I probably should have said so many times during the time we worked together, I am most indebted to my managers who gave me guidance throughout my career including Richard Waterbury, Jay Schuster, and Jerry Colletti.

Also, thank you, Nancy Santos-Ramirez, my assistant, for proofreading and editing my manuscript.

Finally, to my wife, Kathleen, and daughters Diane and Joan . . . thanks for your loving support.

David J. Cichelli
Irvine, California

Preface

Welcome to the powerful—and sometimes confusing—world of sales compensation!

If you are reading this, you probably work with a sales force and your never-ending objective is to help improve sales performance. Your company might be a manufacturer, service provider, reseller, or retailer and your customers may be other businesses or consumers. Your company might sell direct to end users or through channel partners and your sales force might be small or large.

You know that sales compensation is one of many tools available to help you direct your company's sales efforts. You also know that if done correctly, sales compensation can dramatically improve performance and, if done poorly, it can cripple your sales efforts.

Whether you are a sales executive, sales manager, sales operations specialist, finance executive, human resources (HR) compensation manager, information technology (IT) professional, general manager of your division or CEO of your company, you recognize that the goal of increased profitable sales rests squarely with the sales force.

Let's assume you have one of two objectives: You either (1) want to confirm you have a great sales compensation program, or (2) need to develop a new sales compensation plan. This book will provide the answers you seek.

Let's begin:
Sales compensation works!
How salespeople are paid has an immense effect on their performance. With appropriate respect, we will avoid the quagmire of motivational theories that attempt to explain *why* sales compensation works. As any sales manager will attest, salespeople pay very close attention to their sales compensation plan. No, it's not the only reason why sales personnel succeed or fail, but it plays a pivotal role in the overall mix of sales management supervisory tools.

Why This Book

Even though sales compensation is a powerful tool, it can be confusing, too. The setting of target pay, selecting the right performance measures, establishing quotas, determining the mix and upside opportunity, and constructing the right formula are examples of the many choices facing those responsible for crafting the right sales compensation plan. The purpose of this book is to guide you through this effort, helping you make the right choices.

Over the years, I have had the pleasure to teach thousands of professionals how to design and implement successful sales compensation plans. I have also enjoyed the support of my clients as we work together to structure effective sales strategies. You will find other sales compensation books that are informative and helpful, particularly in understanding how strategy drives tactics. This book will take your learning to the next level by showing you how to construct effective sales compensation plans. While it will cover numerous technical topics, it will never stray too far from the practicality of this effort: Sales compensation can significantly affect a company's performance. Of course, it affects people's pay, too. Technical or not, it doesn't get much more personal than that!

How This Book Is Organized

Through the following chapters, you will learn how to construct sales compensation plans that reward sales excellence.

Chapter 1: Why Sales Compensation? Sales compensation helps sales organizations exceed their objectives. However, sales force and sales compensation plans can quickly become outdated. The challenge, as this chapter explains, is to keep the sales compensation plan contemporary with the sales job.

Chapter 2: Sales Compensation Fundamentals. This chapter outlines the basic concepts of sales compensation design. These concepts transcend industries.

Chapter 3: Who Owns Sales Compensation? This chapter explores the process and governance of effective sales compensation.

Chapter 4: Why Job Content Drives Sales Compensation Design. The source of sales compensation design is sales job content—

not industry, not legacy solutions, and not management whim. There are well over 35 different types of sales jobs. We examine several jobs to show how sales compensation varies by sales job type.

Chapter 5: Formula Types. In this chapter, you will find the taxonomy of sales compensation formula types. The chapter provides a hierarchy of formula types, terms, and applications.

Chapter 6: Formula Construction. This chapter describes the methods to construct and calculate formulas for payout purposes. You will need a calculator.

Chapter 7: Support Programs: Territories, Quotas, and Crediting. Sales compensation cannot exist without effective support programs such as quota allocation, sales crediting, and account assignment.

Chapter 8: Administration. Good methods to administer sales compensation programs are necessary so the payouts can be made in a timely and accurate manner. Follow the guidelines presented here to ensure you have the right level of support.

Chapter 9: Implementation and Communication. Rolling out the new plan and ongoing communication helps drive perceived equity into the plan.

Chapter 10: Program Assessment. Is it working or not? A lot of money flows through sales compensation programs. This chapter provides the criteria for judging and improving current programs.

Chapter 11: Sales Compensation Design. This chapter provides the how-to step-by-step approach to redesign the sales compensation plans at your company.

Appendix A provides a sample sales compensation plan. Appendix B is a list of sales compensation surveys. Appendix C provides a list of software vendors.

1

Why Sales Compensation?

The Role of the Sales Force

The role of the sales force is clear. Sell the company's products and services to new and existing customers.

Of course, most of us can easily visualize the "classic" salesperson. Our able and determined salesperson has a geographic territory, travels from one account to another visiting customers and potential buyers, demonstrating the latest gizmo easily drawn from a sample kit or well presented in a glossy brochure. However, this typical image is not fully consistent with today's modern complex sales force. While our fabled territory sales rep is not gone, he or she has been joined by a cadre of sellers. Many companies now sell through multiple sales channels. Our territory rep is now part of a complex customer coverage model that includes telesales, major account sales, product overlay specialists, and partner management. To compound matters, the definition of *products* now varies widely from physical products to services to solutions. To add additional variables, the definition of *sales revenue* has expanded beyond the initial purchase dollars to include rental, lease, product usage revenue, and maintenance revenue. Further, today's sales organizations are often fully integrated with other formerly disconnected customer contact units such as Customer Service, Contracts, Customer Finance, and Collections. In other words, while the classic sales job still exists for many companies, the territory salesperson traveling from one account to another is just one more member of a much more varied and complex sales coverage system.

For convention purposes, we will continue to refer to today's sales coverage system as the "sales force," fully recognizing the expanded characteristics of today's sales departments.

Regardless of the complexity of the sales organization, the sales force continues to serve its primary charter of identifying, securing, and servicing customers. The sales department has at the apex of its objectives what no other department has: the responsibility to manage the profitable revenue growth from the company's customers.

Why Sales Compensation Works

Some nonsalespeople assume sales representatives are solely money motivated. They believe the best (and only way) to manage the sales force is with an overly lucrative sales compensation program. Of course, this is not true. This monetary-centric view of sales representatives promotes a cursory view and inaccurate assumption about sales representatives. It can lead to some false and unfortunate conclusions about the importance of the sales compensation program.

The source of effective management has many competing theories. While the names and themes of these theories might vary, they all subscribe to at least two critical elements: *leadership communication* and *performance measurement.* Great sales compensation plans optimize both of these elements: communication ("this is what's important") and performance measurement ("your incentive payment for last month's performance"). However, clear communication messages and measurement systems don't always fit tidily into a sales compensation plan. There are other and more powerful ways to manage salespeople. For example, day-to-day, hands-on committed sales supervision is considered the best "system" for optimizing sales performance.

A typical conversation between the first-line supervisor and his or her sales charges would sound something like this: "Now, ladies and gentlemen, we are on the line here to achieve this month's sales objectives. I have a commitment from each of you to reach your monthly quota. It's important to me, and it should be important to you. At our next sales meeting, we will put the numbers up on the board to see who we *cheer* and who we *sneer*! If you are having any trouble closing a deal, I can help you. Call me, and we will schedule joint sales calls. Remember, your success is my success!"

This pitch by the first-line supervisor shows the importance of leadership communication (". . . it's important to me, and it should be important to you . . .") and performance measurement (". . . at our next sales meeting, we will put the numbers up on the board to see who we *cheer* and who we *sneer* . . ."). Notice, no mention of money was made, but a heavy dosage of personal accountability and peer pressure is evident.

Interestingly, this vignette illustrates how sales compensation is considered "cross-elastic" with effective sales management. In other words, the better the sales supervision the less the need for aggressive incentive plans to manage sales performance. Further, sales compensation is not a birthright of salespeople. We estimate that 20 percent of all sales personnel are paid with a salary-only program without any variable pay plan.

Regardless of the pay plan, high-performing sales organizations feature ongoing leadership communication and robust performance measurement systems, whether these functions are found in the sales compensation plan or projected through effective sales management, or are a combination of both.

Yes, we agree, the economic transactional value of the incentive compensation dollars *does* provide motivation for increased performance. However, we consider it complementary to other factors such as pride of performance, supervision, affiliation, and goal accomplishment.

Well-run sales departments treat sales compensation as one of several levers of effective management. Along with other management tools, sales compensation can play a contributing role to successful sales production. However, it cannot be the only factor because alone it cannot provide leadership, commitment, and purpose of endeavor that effective sales management can so ideally provide.

The Power of Sales Compensation

A well-designed sales job and sales compensation program can provide dramatic improvement to a company's sales results. When products, customers, sales leadership, jobs, measures, and rewards are in alignment, sales results can be more than remarkable. Sales compensation can provide the right focus on revenue growth, profit improvement, product focus, account penetration, and solution selling.

If sales compensation programs are so powerful, why do they seem to be so "noisy"? In a league of their own, like no other compensation program that the company has, sales compensation programs seem to produce a disproportionate amount of challenges and conflicts. Why is that? There are several reasons. Some issues are to be expected, but others are a result of poor design and poor alignment. Here are examples of some challenges and conflicts:

1. *The chief executive officer (CEO) and the chief financial officer (CFO) are unhappy that the sales compensation program is too*

costly while the company is performing below objective. This is not an uncommon situation. Before concluding that the sales compensation plan is overpaying, you might want to look at the cost of sales. A high cost of sales might be a result of overstaffing and not overpayment to individuals. If actual payouts are too high, then examine the quota system first. Perhaps quotas are too easy.

2. *Product management wants greater product focus from the sales force.* Product managers want to put extra incentives in the sales compensation plan to promote specific products. Product focus is a legitimate measure for sales compensation purposes; however, prior to making changes, product managers have to make good on their own responsibilities, including rationalizing the product offering, segmenting customers, and providing sales messages for unique buyer populations.

3. *Salespeople complain sales quotas are too difficult.* Sales quotas should be difficult. That's their purpose—to stretch performance. Sales compensation is not an appeasement program.

4. *Salespeople seem to ignore components of the sales compensation plan.* This is often the result of a poor sales compensation design, not a motivation issue. A poor design is frequently a reflection of strategy and alignment confusion by senior management. Too many measures, inappropriate measures, or unrealistic objectives will cause sales personnel to ignore one or more components of an incentive plan. Solution: new job definition and a new sales compensation design.

5. *The company spends too much money administering the pay program.* Using low-power tools such as desktop software will cause an increase in headcount for program administration. This may not be the fault of the incentive program, but may be a problem of failing to provide proper information technology (IT) administrative support to the program.

Sales compensation *is* noisy. Sometimes the design is at fault, and sometimes it's an issue of alignment. It can even be just a by-product of an effective program. As a sales compensation designer, this book will help you sort out what problems are real and what are not, where the solution resides, and how to make the right changes.

Job Content—The Source of Sales Compensation Design

When asked about the origin of a sales compensation program within a company, the response might include the following: "It's always been that way" or "It's the industry practice. We follow what others do."

These reasons may sound compelling, but they do not provide a strong rationale for designing effective sales compensation programs. Historical practices, sometimes known as legacy solutions, are often no longer contemporary with market realities or support a sales model that no longer exists.

What about industry practice? Follow industry practice only if your company is identical to your competitors and if they have found the ideal sales compensation solution. However, the likelihood that your products, customers, and customer coverage strategy are identical to your competitors is, at best, remote. So, following what others do in your industry is usually not an effective strategy. As we will learn later, the design of the sales compensation plan is unique to every company.

Effective sales compensation begins with the proper strategy alignment and ends with effective job design. There are several points where sales management *must* achieve alignment before reaching the sales compensation program. The right products must be aligned with the right customers. The right sales jobs must be aligned with the right buyers. The sales jobs must have clarity of purpose—alignment to the sales task—and the performance measures must have alignment with the job content.

Once sales management provides proper alignment among customers, products, and sales jobs, then sales management can craft a sales compensation plan to support the *aligned* sales strategy. As we will learn in Chapter 4, sales compensation design is driven by job content. Get the job right and the sales compensation design is easy. Conversely, create a confusing, misaligned sales job and no sales compensation plan can be successful.

Sales Jobs and Sales Process

The art and science of crafting effective sales compensation programs rest with a commanding competency in sales job design—

assessment, evaluation, and construction. Job design errors are the No. 1 culprit in sales compensation plan failure.

Sales management configures sales jobs to serve a preferred target buyer population. All sales processes comprise five key components. Depending on the products, market, and customers, sales management will define the sales job within the context of these five components:

- *Demand creation:* Stimulating the market

- *Buyer identification:* Finding the decision makers

- *Purchase commitment:* Securing the order

- *Order fulfillment:* Delivering the product or solution

- *Customer support:* Providing ongoing support after the initial purchase

Each step of the selling process contributes to securing and keeping customers. The sales job is often involved in each step of the sales process; however, the level of involvement varies significantly from one company to another and from one sales job to another. The following are descriptions of how sales personnel may be involved in each step.

- *Component 1: Demand Creation:* Typically, the marketing department has responsibility for demand creation. Through advertising, public relations, trade shows, and direct promotion, the marketing department creates demand for the company's products or services. However, in many cases, the sales department will help create demand for the product. This is usually true for companies selling new high-end products in the business-to-business market. This is known as "new market" selling. In these instances, the most practical method to create demand for the product is to hire a seasoned sales force to promote the product to target buyers. In some instances, some sales organizations, such as pharmaceutical sales, only do the first two steps of the sales process—demand creation and buyer identification—with no other sales process responsibility. In these instances, sales personnel promote products but never actually write the order.

- *Component 2: Buyer Identification:* It is normally the responsibility of sales personnel to identify buyers who can make a purchase decision. When selling complex products and services, identifying the buyer(s) can be extremely challenging. Many sales training programs and sales improvement programs spend considerable time educating sales personnel on how to work with the customers' numerous individuals and teams to correctly identify the right decision makers. However, in other companies, marketing, not sales personnel, assumes responsibility for both demand creation *and* buyer identification by having customers identify themselves through direct response either by mail, telephone, or Web site visits. Finally, in other companies, the marketing department is responsible for identifying potential buyers through research conducted by telemarketing reps. Marketing then assigns these potential buyers (hot leads) to the sales force for sales efforts.

- *Component 3: Purchase Commitment:* The primary value of a sales representative is to secure a purchase commitment from a customer. This step is typically known as "closing" the sale. We all share a common image of a sales rep opening up the order book and writing down the customer's order. (This is how the now seemingly quaint expression "book the order" came into the sales world vernacular.) While a high-tech version of booking the order still exists today, securing a purchase commitment can be an involved and complex process of contracts, fulfillment obligations, performance-pricing, and delivery commitments. For most companies, a booked order now arrives via an electronic medium. Still, some sales departments require their sales personnel to remain involved in every part of the transaction, ensuring that all elements of the purchase process have been successfully completed. At the other end of the spectrum, we find customers so well acquainted with products that they do not need or want a salesperson involved in the purchase process. These customers prefer to order by telephone, fax, or from an e-commerce Web site.

- *Component 4: Order Fulfillment:* The actual delivery of a product or service to a customer is collectively called *order fulfillment.* In some cases, the salesperson provides order fulfillment, but frequently this responsibility rests with others. But there are many selling models where sales organizations require sales personnel to oversee the successful delivery of the product to the customer. Customers will typically call the salesperson to check on the status of the order as they await delivery or ask for assistance if there is an order fulfillment problem.

- *Component 5: Customer Service:* Most sales organizations work collaboratively with customer service departments to provide after-the-sale support. Even so, sales representatives will occasionally find themselves involved in customer service issues if a customer is not satisfied with a product or service. In some companies, this is a mandated part of the sales job, and sales personnel will work with internal resources to ensure customer satisfaction.

Each of these activities—demand creation, buyer identification, purchase commitment, order fulfillment, and customer service—contribute to a successful sales process. The role of the salesperson will vary depending on products, customers, and the company's sales coverage model. The mix and configuration of these sales process roles determine the content of the sales job, and sales job content drives sales compensation design.

Sales Compensation—Paying for the Point of Persuasion

The highest value provided by sales personnel is to help customers make choices when there is uncertainty and risk. This event is known as the *point of persuasion*. The purpose of sales compensation is to reward seller success at the point of persuasion.

While salesperson involvement in the sales process will vary from one sales job to another, the task of building the right sales compensation plan is greatly simplified by looking for the point of persuasion.

In most cases, we will find that the point of persuasion is at the *Purchase Commitment* sales process step, but not always. For example, the point of persuasion might be in the first step, *Demand Creation*, where the salesperson's point of persuasion is to cause the customer to learn more about a company's products. Conversely, it might be at a later stage in the sales process, such as at *Order Fulfillment*, when a customer is having second thoughts about the purchase and the salesperson must reassure the customer of the wisdom of the purchase. *Finding, defining, and measuring the point of persuasion is the focus of effective sales compensation design.*

Sales Force Obsolescence and Sales Compensation

Maintaining alignment and avoiding obsolescence is the continuing struggle of sales leadership. Sales force obsolescence is a natural occurrence for all sales departments. Over a period of time, most sales forces will become obsolete. By this, we do not mean that *salespeople* will become obsolete. It is the sales department (its strategy and its deployment model) that becomes obsolete. The outcome of accumulated misalignment among products, customers, and sales resources produces an obsolete sales force.

With this obsolescence, the point of persuasion can change, shift, or be diminished. To illustrate this point, consider the following question: "Would you buy a commercial poster/print of birds over the Internet?" Most people would answer this question, "Yes." The reason they would buy a print over the Internet is because they understand what a print is and its value. They certainly don't need the assistance of a salesperson. However, when the question is modified, people are not so sure they would buy a print over the Internet without the aid of a salesperson. For example, consider this restated question: "As your first investment in rare prints of birds, would you purchase a John James Audubon print from The Havell Edition of "Birds of America" over the Internet? Many people would answer, "No." Why would they answer, "No"? In one case, a person is willing to buy a print over the Internet; yet in another case the same person is not willing. The answer is simple. There is risk and uncertainty in purchasing a rare print. Until you have the personal expertise to reduce your risk and uncertainty, you will seek the assistance of an adviser such as an informed and respected salesperson.

Here is another example: Would you buy a personal computer over the phone or via an e-commerce Web site? Today, many longtime PC users purchase their computers without the assistance of a salesperson. However, when these same individuals were making their first PC purchase, they sought the advice and assurance of salespeople before they made their purchase decision.

So, salespeople are ideally suited to be at the point where customers have risk and uncertainty—at the point of persuasion. As illustrated above, this point of persuasion is constantly on the move. Sales organizations and sales jobs can become obsolete as the point of persuasion moves beyond the current deployment model.

A dated coverage model nearly dooms an encyclopedia company. An encyclopedia company was late to realize that its sales coverage model was going to doom the company. *The selling of encyclopedias has a long and proud history of providing personal in-home sales contact to parents looking to acquire additional educational support for their children. Expensive, with annual updates*

and custom furniture, a multivolume encyclopedia was tradition-
ally a significant purchase. The company's authorized in-home
sales agents sold within exclusive territories. The company provided
no other channel to buy the product. The company was loyal to its
agents—to a fault. As parents became more sophisticated, the rise
of mega bookstores offering multivolume encyclopedias occurred.
New competitors entered the market including CD encyclopedias,
and the in-house sales agents became a sales coverage liability.
Long past the point of obvious need for change, the company aban-
doned its use of a single sales channel, almost too late. Preferred So-
lution: monitor sales coverage models actively. Preclude sales chan-
nel obsolescence by moving quickly to keep sales personnel aligned
with buyer populations.

The Impact of Customer Relationship Management

The promise of customer relationship management (CRM) is to provide a single-technology platform for tracking and managing the sales
process. With a common technology platform, CRM offers the opportunity for assigning and managing elements of the sales process continuum to divergent parties while successfully keeping track of all
customer interactions. In this respect, CRM can alter sales job content.
As a company shifts parts of the sales process to other resources, what
role does the salesperson perform? Remember, the definition of this
revised job role is the starting point for effective sales compensation
design.

Summary

Sales compensation works as part of a complex management process.
Look to job content as the source for designing effective sales compensation plans. Locate the point of persuasion and reward the salesperson for making a difference—that is where sales compensation
belongs.

2

Sales Compensation Fundamentals

In this chapter, we will review key sales compensation fundamentals. First, we will review variable compensation models and then examine why sales compensation is unique. Next, we will discuss the difference between income producers and sales representatives. Lastly, we will examine sales compensation design elements.

Variable Compensation Models

Figure 2-1 depicts four different types of common variable compensation models.

The horizontal line reflects the target total cash compensation (TTCC) for the job. We depict the base salary amount as dark shading while variable dollars have no shading. Note that the first two variable compensation methods—Gainsharing and Add-on—have a full base salary with no variable pay below TTCC. In the remaining two types—Management Bonus and Sales Compensation—the base salary amount is less than the TTCC amount. We refer to this difference as the target incentive or the at-risk dollars.

The characteristics and application of these four common pay systems differ from one another.

- *Gainsharing:* Corporate gainsharing plans help drive overall corporate success by tying payouts to corporate results. Gainsharing plans have no pay at risk and therefore present no downside cost to the employee. Most corporate gainsharing plans tie payouts to a percentage of corporate revenue or profit. In this manner, management shares the incremental gain with employees on a prespecified proportional basis. Sometimes local management will use a gainsharing plan to help boost productivity. Generally, all employees participate in the gainsharing plan with no restriction on the number of employees who can receive a payout. Normally, participants earn no

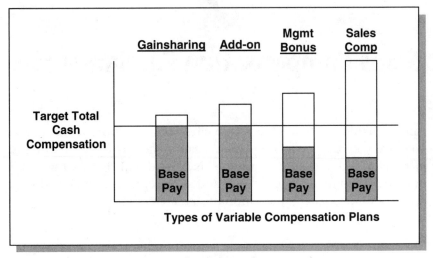

Figure 2-1. Types of Variable Compensation Plans

payout unless the company or unit reaches its stated goal. Gainsharing plans target between 3 and 8 percent of base salary for payout purposes, although this number varies by company and wage inflation trends. These programs tend to surge in popularity every 10 to 15 years. Gainsharing plans have a mixed history of success. The most successful programs succeed as a result of high-level commitment by corporate leadership. Unfortunately, gainsharing plans fail when participants view the program as an entitlement. An entitlement perspective produces the following results: Payouts in good years garner only modest satisfaction, while no payouts in bad years produce significant dissatisfaction.

- *Add-on programs:* Management uses add-on pay plans in a variety of circumstances. While gainsharing plans tend to be all-inclusive, add-on plans target specific work units, jobs, or people. Add-on plans provide a target dollar earning or a target percentage of base salary for accomplishment of preestablished goals. Some add-on plans are permanent and ongoing, for example, "10 percent of base salary paid to the most productive top 10 percent of customer service representatives." Other add-on plans serve short-term purposes such as contests and special program incentive funds (SPIFs). They fit numerous situations and provide additional pay for individual or unit performance. Payouts occur only for above-goal performance and average 5 to 10 percent of base salaries. While normally very effective, add-on plans have downside risks. Too many duplicate plans, excessive payments, inappropriate goals, and inconsistent eligibility criteria can weaken add-on plans.

- *Management bonus plans:* Most companies provide a management bonus opportunity for director-level jobs and above. Stated as a percentage of base salary, management bonus targets vary from as low as 10 percent of base salary to as high as 100 percent of base salary, depending on the job level—in other words, the higher the position, the higher the target bonus percentage. Target bonus and target base salary combine to equal total target cash compensation with payouts tied to a combination of business unit, corporate, and individual performance results. Participants can earn payouts for below-target performance. Management bonus plans normally provide twice the target earnings as an upside opportunity for outstanding performance known as a double upside incentive opportunity. Most management bonus plans have a high performance threshold and usually don't have any restriction on the number of participants who receive a payout, but most plans cap the upside incentive payout.

- *Sales compensation:* Sales compensation is different from gainsharing, add-on plans, and management bonus programs. Only sales personnel (and their managers) participate in the sales compensation program. Two criteria define a sales job: (1) The job incumbent must have customer contact, and (2) The primary role of the incumbent is to persuade the customer to act. Sales compensation plans tie performance measures to individual or sales teams' efforts. Sales compensation is available for two types of sellers: income producers and sales representatives:

  • *Income producers:* An income producer's actions create business revenue. Examples include real-estate agents, stockbrokers, insurance agents, currency and bond traders, manufacturer representatives, and mortgage origination specialists. In essence, income producers are mini-business units. Their value is not in the products they offer, but the relationships they manage. Often, the products they represent are commodities and are sold by numerous people. What is unique is their relationship with their customers; they often have the power to take their customers with them when they change employers. Typically, income producers have no base salary and are paid a flat commission rate on sales. Although management may identify a preferred earnings level, the percentage of sales dollars is a more important consideration. Income producers evaluate the competitiveness of pay by the size of the commission rate.

- *Sales representatives:* A sales representative *represents* the value of his or her company's products, services, and solutions. The inherent value of the relationship between the company and its customer rests with the company's value proposition. It's the role of the sales representative to present this value proposition to all customers to affect sales. The ratio between base salary and target incentive pay as a portion of TTCC varies by job content. The more the salesperson can influence a customer to act, the lower the base salary as a portion of target total cash compensation and the higher the at-risk component. The opposite is also true: The less personal influence inherent in a sales job to affect customer buying decisions, the higher the base salary and the lower the incentive opportunity. Upside earning opportunities are set at 3 times the at-risk component; thus the payout level for outstanding performance is known as a "triple." Performance measures are tied to sales production. Payouts begin below target performance and may or may not have a performance threshold. A preferred performance distribution features two-thirds reaching and exceeding quota and one-third not reaching quota. Sales management helps achieve this performance distribution through effective quota setting. While pay caps are generally avoided, fewer than 10 percent of individuals usually exceed the triple upside earnings level. Management accomplishes this control of upside earnings through sound formula construction and effective quota assignment. When communicating to participants, sales management presents the compensation program as a base salary (if present) plus an incentive formula.

Income Producers versus Sales Representatives

It is easy to confuse the income producers with sales representatives and vice versa. Income producers and sales representatives are very much alike. They sell products to customers. They both earn incentive compensation for sales results. They even share similar commission formula types. However, the underlying economic principles differ between income producers and sales representatives. Income producers split a portion of their commission—sales transaction earnings—with their employer. For example, stockbrokers earn a commission on every buy or sell transaction. Part of the commission is paid to the stockbroker—the income producer—and part to the brokerage house. Often, income producers receive no base salary or a modest draw. Sales revenue provides the funding for income producer payments. Competitiveness of pay is evaluated by comparing commission rates, and actual compensation levels are less relevant. In fact, employers encourage high earnings as additional dollars are shared between the employer and the income producer. The more the income producer makes, the more the company makes. Scant attention is given to high or low payments. Over the long run, macro labor market trends make adjustments to income producers' earnings by increasing or decreasing the number of income producers working in the market, and, as a result, employment levels closely mimic the expansion and contraction of income producer markets.

On the other hand, the underlying economic model for sales representatives differs from income producers. Sales management identifies a TTCC and performance expectations for the sales representative job. Sales management calibrates incentive formula and quota levels to ensure that payouts conform to expected performance distribution for minimal, target, and outstanding pay expectations.

Whereas income producers' pay levels are managed by sales production multiplied by the commission rate, the sales representative's pay is always managed as compared to a preferred target compensation level. As a sales representative performs against target performance, a portion of the incentive compensation is awarded—low performance earns low pay, and high performance earns high pay—all measured in relation to the target incentive amount.

The relationship of pay and sales volume is usually linear for income producers. As Figure 2-2 illustrates, the more products sold, the higher the payout.

However, the relationship between earnings and volume is not linear for sales representatives as shown in Figure 2-3. Earnings increase as sales volume increases, but at a decreasing rate.

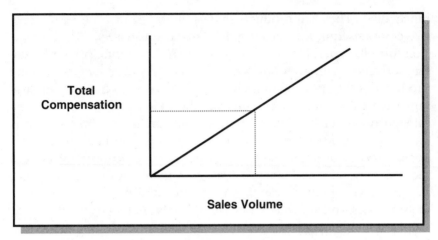

Figure 2-2. Income Producer—Sales Volume and Pay

When compared to Figure 2-4, the pay lines for income producers and sales representatives clearly differ.

Labor market practices continue to provide higher pay levels for sales representatives, but at a decreasing rate as compared to depending on the volume of sales production. This mathematical rela-

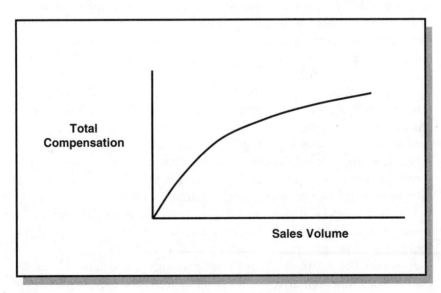

Figure 2-3. Sales Representative—Sales Volume and Pay

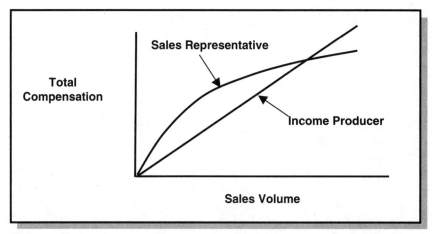

Figure 2-4. Sales Representative and Income Producer—Sales Volume and Pay

tionship is often embedded in the job family structure. Figure 2-5 demonstrates that pay continues to increase in each job, but at a decreasing rate.

We will examine more income producer pay issues later in the book. Let's now return to sales representative issues.

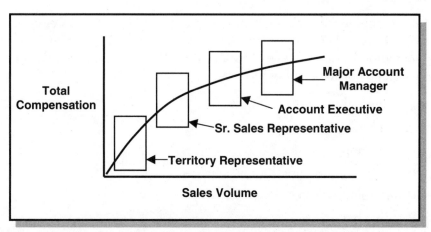

Figure 2-5. Sales Representative—Sales Volume and Pay by Job

About Sales Compensation Concepts

In this next section, you will find highlighted boxes featuring sales compensation concepts. Each concept states a best-practice solution.

> **Key Concept: Sales Representatives Self-Fund Their Sales Compensation Payments.** While sales revenue funds sales compensation payments for income producers, sales representatives fund their own sales compensation program. This occurs as the sales compensation program redistributes the at-risk monies. Better performers make more than their target at-risk incentive pay, and poor performers make less than their at-risk target incentive pay. While the math does not always fit perfectly—sometimes more is paid, sometimes less is paid—the concept is clear: Sales representatives collectively fund their sales compensation plan through redistribution of the target at-risk incentive compensation dollars based on performance.

The remaining material in this chapter addresses design elements for sales representatives. We will revisit sales compensation design choices in Chapter 5, "Formula Types."

Sales Compensation Design Elements for Sales Representatives

Sales compensation design elements are the building blocks of effective sales compensation plans. Each sales compensation plan is the summation of decisions made about these design elements. The design elements are as follows:

- Eligibility
- Target total compensation
- Pay mix and leverage
- Performance measures and weights
- Quotas distribution
- Performance range
- Performance and payment periods

Decisions about these design elements must be made before selecting the appropriate formula.

All sales compensation plans for sales representative jobs share these same design elements. A company can build a coherent overall sales compensation program by adopting one set of design principles for all design elements. Sales management can then apply these design principles to all sales jobs when building job-specific sales compensation plans. In this manner, sales management creates a sales compensation program comprising individual sales compensation plans; yet each plan is consistent with the company's design principles.

> **Key Concept: Sales Compensation Plans Should Equal the Number of Sales Jobs.** Sales compensation follows sales job design. Sales compensation supports the sales management objectives for each sales job. Sales compensation plans are not designed for individual salespeople unless the individual is a single incumbent for a job. The number of unique sales compensation plans should be equal to the number of unique sales jobs.

Eligibility

Which jobs should be eligible for sales compensation? There are many different types of jobs within the sales department. Not all of them should be eligible for sales compensation plan participation. Establishing a job eligibility policy will resolve confusion regarding which jobs and their incumbents should participate in the sales compensation program. This decision about sales compensation plan eligibility does not preclude noneligible jobs and their incumbents from participating in other incentive plans such as gainsharing, add-on plans, and management bonus plans. The most common eligibility criteria require job incumbents to (1) have customer contact and (2) persuade the customer to act in a positive financial benefit to the company. Of course this would include salespeople, telesales, channel sales representatives, and many other customer contact personnel. It would usually exclude such jobs as the district manager's secretary or headquarters' product managers.

However, companies do adopt different practices than the one stated above. Some companies are more expansive with their eligibility rules and other companies are more restrictive. Regardless, a company needs to establish the criteria for sales compensation eligibility. Absent such a policy, ongoing confusion about which jobs are or are not eligible for sales compensation will arise.

Sample Eligibility Policy: *For a job to be eligible to participate in the sales compensation program, the incumbents must (1) have customer contact and (2) persuade the customer to act with a positive financial benefit to the company.*

   Your Eligibility Policy:

_____

_____

Target Total Cash Compensation

Sales personnel who reach expected performance earn target total cash compensation (TTCC). Depending on individual performance, some sales representatives will earn more and some will earn less.

   Using survey data and applying management judgment, management establishes a TTCC for each job.

   The total remuneration for sales jobs includes the following cash and noncash components:

- *Base salary:* Most sales representatives receive a base salary.

- *Sales compensation:* Sales compensation is the variable pay tied to sales performance.

- *Benefits:* Sales representatives participate in the company's benefit programs.

- *Contests/SPIFs:* Management uses add-on contests and SPIFs to reward special efforts.

- *Recognition events:* Most companies provide a special annual recognition event for outstanding salespeople.

- *Expense reimbursement:* Expense reimbursement pays out-of-pocket costs of sales representatives.

Target total cash compensation includes both the base salary and the sales compensation components. It excludes benefits, contests and/or SPIFs, recognition events, and sales expense reimbursement.

Key Concept: Don't Overpay or Underpay for Sales Performance. For sales representatives, don't significantly overpay or underpay for sales performance as compared to market practices. High pay will incur excessive sales costs, while underpayment will escalate costs in other areas such as low productivity, turnover, and poor morale. Ensure market comparisons are consistent with the range of sales performance by matching expected payouts to the survey data for the 25th, 50th, and 75th percentile of market payout amounts.

Setting the correct TTCC requires collecting accurate external pay data and making judgments regarding internal equity among all the sales jobs, and perhaps other jobs within the company.

Some companies prefer to take a more aggressive competitive pay position as compared to labor market rates, while others prefer to be more conservative. Regardless, sales management needs to review and manage TTCC consistently from year to year. This includes capturing external labor market data from reliable survey sources on an annual basis and making necessary adjustments to target pay levels.

Sample Target Total Cash Compensation Policy: Set the TTCC for each job at the 60th percentile of market practices as presented in the annual [xyz] industry survey. Payouts for poor performers will be equal to the 25th percentile of pay; top performers will earn payouts equal to or greater than the 90th percentile of labor market rates.

Your Target Total Cash Compensation Policy:

Pay Mix and Leverage

Pay mix and leverage together provide the range of pay opportunities based on sales performance.

- *Pay mix:* Pay mix splits TTCC into two components: base salary and target incentive amount. We express pay mix as a percentage split with the first number representing the base salary and the second number representing the target incentive amount:

Base Salary/Target Incentive
These two amounts added together always equal 100 percent.

Examples:	**90/10**	Base Salary = 90% of TTCC
		Target Incentive = 10% of TTCC
	75/25	Base Salary = 75% of TTCC
		Target Incentive = 25% of TTCC

For a TTCC of $100,000, the 90/10 pay mix provides a target base salary of $90,000 and a target incentive opportunity of $10,000. A pay mix of 75/25 for the same TTCC of $100,000 provides a target base salary of $75,000 and a target incentive opportunity of $25,000.

Pay mix varies by job content. Generally, as the relative influence of the sales representative increases, the lower the base salary component and the higher the target incentive amount. For example, a new account territory sales job might have a pay mix of 60/40 whereas a major account sales job might have a pay mix of 80/20. The average pay mix for business-to-business territory sales representatives in the United States is approximately 70/30. However, there is a wide variance to this national norm.

Figure 2-6 shows different levels of pay mix with 100/0 having no pay at risk and 0/100 with 100 percent of the TTCC at risk.

- *Leverage:* Leverage is a mathematical expression for the upside earning potential for a sales job. We express leverage as a multiplier of the target incentive. The most common leverage is known as a "triple." For notation purposes, it is normally written as "3x." Do not confuse leverage as a pay cap. The leverage amount provides an upside earnings estimate for the best performers. For definition purposes, we define *best performers* as the 90th percentile of performance among all job incumbents. In other words, the best performers receive three times the target incentive for outstanding sales performance, defined as the 90th percentile of sales personnel for that job.

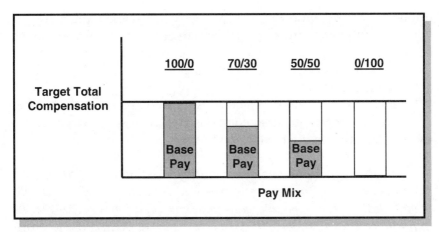

Figure 2-6. Pay Mix Examples

The triple rule of leverage (3x) is a shorthand method to replicate what takes place in the labor market. However, certain companies will intentionally pay more than a triple leverage, such as 3.5x or 4x, to provide more aggressive pay for their top performers. Or they will pay less than a triple leverage—2.5x for their top performers—presuming the labor market does not support a 3x for the best performers. The company does not need to pay market pay levels. As with any target pay level, management judgment is the ultimate source for setting

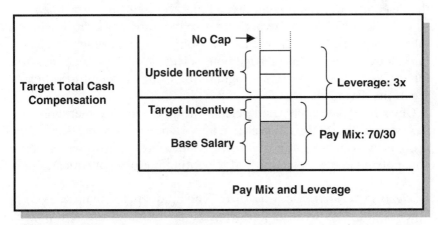

Figure 2-7. Pay Mix and Leverage

upside incentive opportunity. However, labor market practices for 75th and 90th percentile of the labor market pay levels provide an excellent reference point for evaluating a proposed leverage.

Pay mix and leverage provide the range of pay opportunities available to sales personnel.

Figure 2-7 shows the complete relationship among the following components: target total cash compensation, base salary, target incentive, upside incentive, pay mix, and leverage.

Sample Pay Mix and Leverage Policy: Each job has its own pay mix depending on the degree of personal influence configured into the job design. Territory sales jobs will have a pay mix of 70/30 and major account sales jobs will have a pay mix of 80/20. The leverage for individual contributor sales territory jobs will be 3x, overlay specialists 2.75x, and first-line sales supervisors 2.5x. The leverage for new market sellers is 3.5x.

Your Pay Mix and Leverage Policy:

_____

_____

Performance Measures and Weights

The art of designing effective sales compensation formulas rests with the discipline of selecting and weighting the right performance measures. The selection of the performance measures for inclusion in the sales compensation plan marks the point where strategy translates into tactics. When sales management selects a performance measure for the sales compensation program, then sales leadership officially sanctions that measure.

Once the leadership team selects the performance measures, the next step is to establish the relative importance of each measure. This is done by weighting the performance measures. Below, we examine concepts related to selecting and weighting performance measures.

- *Selecting performance measures:* The uniqueness of any sales compensation rests with its performance measures. There are dozens of different types of performance measures, but the most common and most practical fall into four major categories:

- *Volume production measures:* Volume production measures are the most popular and appropriate performance measures for sales compensation purposes. Production measures include three categories: sales revenue (purchase, continuing, renewed, and estimated), profit dollars (gross margin, contribution margin), and items (units, contracts, and design-wins).
- *Sales effectiveness measures:* Sales effectiveness measures help improve sales results by focusing sales efforts in the areas of product (balance, mix, launch, cross-sell, packages, solutions), accounts (new, retained, penetrate, growth, win-back), orders (close rate, size, length of contract, linearity, and receivables), and price management (discounts, rebates, realization, and percent change).
- *Customer impact measures:* Customer impact measures evaluate sales satisfaction (customer surveys, number of complaints) and loyalty (order persistency, market share, and comparative loyalty survey scores).
- *Resource utilization measures:* Resource utilization measures confirm the effective use of resources includes the following measures: productivity (cost per order dollar, quota sales loading), channels (partner success, partner participation rates, outlet performance), and subordinates (for supervisors—balance performance, turnover, and new hire ramp rate).

> **Key Concept: Use No More Than Three Output Measures in a Sales Compensation Plan.** Sales compensation plans work best with three or fewer performance measures. Limiting performance measures ensures that those selected get the full attention of the sales force. Use output measures tied to actual sales results and avoid input measures such as presales activity measures (e.g., number of sales calls or proposal written).

- *Weighting performance measures:* Senior management confirms the importance of each performance measure by allocating a portion of 100 percent to each of the measures.

Performance Measures

	Sales volume	Product mix	Retention
Weighting:	**55%**	**25%**	**20%**

No single measure should be worth less than 15 percent. The summation of the weights always equals 100 percent. Each job has its own unique set of performance measures and weights.

Sample Performance Selection and Weighting Policy: A sales compensation plan will have three or fewer output performance measures. No measure will be worth less than 15 percent of the total weighting. The primary measure of sales success is net sales revenue performance less service contract revenue. All plans will have a customer loyalty measure representing 15 percent of the value of the incentive plan.

Your Performance Selection and Weighting Policy:

Quota Distribution

Quota distribution establishes the desired difficulty of quotas. If quotas are too easy, the sales compensation plan might overpay. If quotas are too difficult, the sales compensation program could underpay. A preferred quota distribution target is to have two-thirds of the salespeople reaching and exceeding quota and one-third not. This distribution of performance allows for the cross-funding of upside pay to high performers by shifting a share of the low performers' target incentive pay to the better performers.

This distribution of two-thirds over quota and one-third below quota is a target distribution outcome. In some years, the distribution may be skewed in one direction or the other. However, over the long run the distribution should favor the split of two-thirds exceeding quota and one-third not exceeding quota.

Figure 2-8 shows this preferred two-thirds reaching and exceeding quota and one-third not reaching quota.

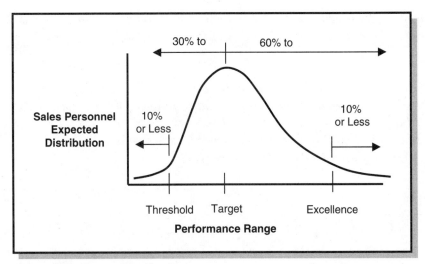

Figure 2-8. Quota Distribution

A more mathematically rigorous model might suggest a target of 50/50 quota distribution, with 50 percent exceeding quota and 50 percent not reaching quota to ensure that the cross-funding of below-quota performers and above-quota performers is in balance. However, due to the use of thresholds and the impact of terminations, the two-thirds versus one-third model seems to provide the right cross-funding balance.

Record breaking unit sales, bad quota performance. The sales force for a contact lens company had broken all unit sales records. However, the VP of Sales had to contend with a morale problem because only 5 percent of the sales personnel reached sales revenue quota. *Even though the company was being lauded for its sales powerlessness, fewer than 5 percent of sales personnel would earn target incentive pay. A price war on contact lenses ignited dramatic sales growth. Because quotas were established and measured in revenue, sales success—defined as revenue performance—dropped as the company took substantial market share by using a low price strategy. They sold a lot more lenses at lower prices, but still did not hit their revenue goals. High unit sales success could not offset the lower price per unit. Sales personnel could not reach their sales revenue goals. Preferred Solution: The basic assumptions about the incentive plan* *were negated when the price of the product collapsed. Terminate the old plan and redesign a new plan to match the company's new market dynamics.*

Sample Quota Distribution Policy: *The summation of all quota assignments should equal the company budget forecast. Quota distribution targets two-thirds of all sales personnel for a job to reach and exceed quota, and one-third not to reach quota.*
Your Quota Distribution Policy:

_____

_____

Performance Range

Performance range specifies the low and high spread of performance for payment purposes. The low point of this range represents minimal performance where performance below this level should not receive incentive payment. The high point of this range represents excellent performance where outstanding performance should receive outstanding pay such as 3x leverage. The performance range of a measure differs from one measure to another, from one job to another, from one company to another, and from one industry to another. As an example, the performance range for an established consumer product is normally very narrow. Salespeople will find it unlikely to sell above 105 percent of goal. Likewise, the chance of falling below 95 percent of goal is also remote. Mature consumer products have a very predictable and narrow performance range. However, new growth industries might have a very wide performance range. As an example, sales of 200 percent over goal might be the norm for exceptional performance while 50 percent of goal might be considered typical minimal performance. Each performance measure has its own performance range. Sales management can best determine the performance range for a given measure by examining its historical range.

In Figure 2-9A, the performance range is from 70 to 145 percent. Low performers (10th percentile) perform at or below 70 percent to quota. Excellent performers achieve 145 percent of quota where the

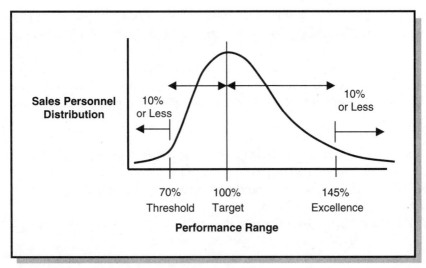

Figure 2-9A. Performance Range—Example A

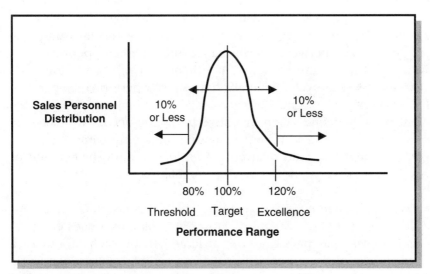

Figure 2-9B. Performance Range—Example B

top 10th percentile will perform and should receive outstanding pay.

In Figure 2-9B, the performance range is 80 percent for low performers and 120 percent for excellent performers.

Sales management needs to identify the performance range for each measure in each sales compensation plan. As we learn later, we will use this information to build the sales compensation formula rates.

Sample Performance Range Policy: Threshold and excellence performance levels will be set for each performance measure. Threshold reflects the lower 10 percent of performance, and excellence represents the top 10 percent of performance.

Your Performance Range Policy:

_____

_____

Performance and Payment Periods

Performance periods and payment periods work together. Sales management sets the performance period for each formula measure—the length of time between performance measurement periods. This window of time can be a week, month, quarter, or even as long as a year. Shorter sales cycles generally have shorter performance periods; longer sales cycles generally have longer performance periods. Payment periods define when incentive payments occur. Normally, the performance period and the payment period are the same, for example, measured and paid quarterly. Additionally, performance and/or payment periods can be discrete or cumulative.

- *Discrete:* Discrete performance/payment periods stand alone for measurement and payment purpose. For example, a sales compensation plan that pays "monthly discrete" treats each month as a standalone measurement and payment period. No previous or future month's performance will affect the payout for an individual month. Use less than annual discrete measurement periods when sales cycles are short and sales personnel have no flexibility or self-serving motivation to move orders from one period to another.

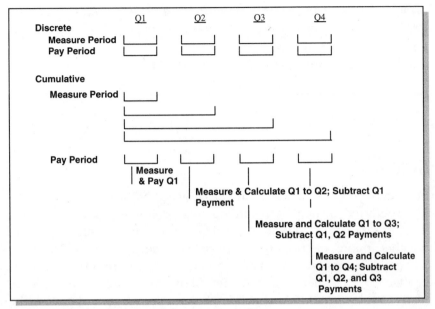

Figure 2-10. Performance/Payment Periods

- *Cumulative:* Use a cumulative performance/payment period when you want the salesperson to be paid at more frequent intervals than the ultimate measurement period. As an example, "paid quarterly on cumulative year-to-date performance" provides payouts each quarter based on year-to-date performance.

Figure 2-10 displays both discrete and cumulative performance measurement and payment periods.

As the cumulative period to date performance/payment periods demonstrate in Figure 2-10, the salesperson always carries the responsibility for year-to-date performance even though payouts are being made on a quarterly basis. Each quarter, the year-to-date performance and incentive are calculated. To make the quarterly payments, any previous quarterly payments are subtracted from this year-to-date amount before the final payment for the quarter is made.

A sales compensation plan might have several formula components. Some might be paid with a discrete performance/payment period while others might be paid with a cumulative period-to-date performance/payment period.

Sample Performance/Payment Period Policy: Sales personnel are responsible for year-to-date sales performance. More frequent payouts can be made on a cumulative year-to-date basis.
　Your Performance/Payment Period Policy:

_____

_____

Summary

To effectively manage sales compensation, a company needs to establish preferred principles regarding plan eligibility, target total cash compensation, pay mix and leverage, performance measures and weights, quota distribution, performance range, and performance and payment periods. As markets, products, and corporate objectives change, so will sales jobs and their supporting sales compensation plans. By documenting the company's overriding principles, the process of sales compensation design should create plan designs consistent with corporate principles, but aligned with sales unit goals.

3

Who Owns Sales Compensation?

"Who owns the sales compensation program?" might seem like an academic question to some. "The sales department" is the obvious answer; yet when we examine this issue more closely, we find many players are involved in the design and management of the sales compensation program. Sales wants to drive performance. Marketing and product management wants focus on select products. Finance wants a fiscally responsible pay program. The human resource department wants total target cash compensation (TTCC) to be externally competitive and internally equitable with nonsales jobs. The information technology (IT) department wants to provide timely and accurate administrative support and legal wants legally protected and compliant pay programs. Not surprisingly, the CEO of the company wants the sales compensation program to support the strategy of each business unit.

In a recent study* by The Alexander Group, Inc., and *Sales and Marketing Management* magazine, 590 companies responded to this question: "The ultimate authority for sales compensation plan resides with. . ."

42.6%	Sales Management/Sales Operations
35.6%	CEO/General Manager
10.6%	HR/Compensation
4.6%	Finance
0.9%	Marketing
5.7%	Other

*2003 Sales Compensation Trends Survey[©]

While the survey responses support the sales management as the ultimate authority, note the involvement of the chief executive officer (CEO)/general manager. Even after eliminating the statistical impact of small sales forces from the survey data, the CEO/general manager is still the ultimate authority for the sales compensation plan for

25 percent of the reporting sales organizations having more than 100 sales representatives.

The sales compensation program (base salary and incentive payments) helps drive revenue growth but also represents a significant financial cost to the company. For a sales force of more than 100 eligible employees, the sales compensation program can have an annual budget between $10 and $20 million. The accountable revenues can be between $100 and $250 million—and the larger the sales force, the larger the costs and attendant revenue commitment. The point is sales compensation budgets are large, their revenue impact is significant, and they require active management—by multiple parties—to be successful.

Sales Compensation Program Ownership

Although the sales compensation program must serve many (and often competing) objectives, it is still a sales management program. It is part of an array of management tools used by the sales department to manage sales productivity. It does not sit independent of a fully integrated sales management model. We suggest that the sales department act as the steward of the sales compensation program. But others, such as the CEO/general manager, marketing, finance, and human resources, must have access to the design, management, and administration of the sales compensation program.

In this chapter, we present sales compensation program accountabilities and suggest appropriate program responsibilities—who should do what to make sure the sales compensation program works effectively.

Program Accountabilities

The following program accountabilities support successful management of the sales compensation program:

- *Strategic alignment:* As corporate objectives migrate regarding markets, products, revenue growth, and profit goals, sales management must continually update the sales department to support these changing business objectives. Sometimes, major changes in strategy require major organizational changes creating new sales entities, new jobs, and new accountabilities. Other changes might be more subtle and can be made within the context of the existing sales organization. Whether the changes are major or minor, sales management, in most cases, must realign the sales compensation program to support new goals. Ongoing strategic realignment of the sales compensation program caused by changing corporate objectives confirms the need for periodic review and update of the sales compensation plans.

- *Effective design:* Sales compensation plans have numerous features and components. An effective design will properly support strategic objectives of the company and work correctly by providing the right payouts for different levels of actual performance. Additionally, all sales compensation plans must work in concert with one another so that the overall sales compensation program (including crediting practices, quota allocation, and account assignments policies) works in logical unison. An effective sales compensation design ensures that all program features and components work together correctly.

- *Plan management:* Communication, training, interpretations, and adjustments are part of successful sales compensation program management. Plan rollout is the primary communication event for the sales compensation program. Communication also includes documentation, promotion, and feedback, and easy access via dedicated Web sites. New hires and newly appointed sales managers need training on the application of the sales compensation program. Plan provision interpretation occurs regularly due to unforeseen events, and minor design issues and adjustments will occasionally need to be made to fix problems.

- *Program administration:* Day-to-day administration of the program ensures proper sales crediting, payroll payment files, and management reporting.

- *Program assessment:* Regular assessment tests the sales compensation program for success. Numerous assessment methods examine strategic intent, competitiveness of pay, management utility, and sales force motivation.

- *Audit and legal review:* Finance audits and legal reviews keep the sales compensation program compliant with company guidelines and policies.

Whether you have a sales department of five sales representatives or a large sales department of 5,000 sales representatives, each of the above-mentioned program accountabilities exists in your organization. Someone has to do each of these tasks. For a small sales force, it might be the CEO or the vice president of sales doing them all. In larger sales organizations, these tasks are allocated to various parties as we describe in the next section.

Assignment of Program Accountabilities—Large Sales Organizations

The following presents possible accountability assignments by job role. While this is not a prescriptive model, it does provide an outline of traditional responsibilities for large sales departments. ("Large," in this case, means more than 200 sales personnel.)

- *CEO/Business unit general manager:* The CEO/business unit general manager must articulate the business objectives and goals to the sales department. The business unit manager must also approve final plan designs to ensure alignment with business objectives and goals.

- *Vice president of sales:* The vice president (VP) of sales has overall responsibility for the sales compensation program. With the sales management leadership team, the VP of sales determines the proper role for sales compensation in the mix of the sales management model. Final accountability for sales compensation program effectiveness rests with the VP of sales.

- *VP of marketing:* The vice president of marketing provides information about product strategy and customer segments. The VP of marketing also needs to confirm that the sales compensation program correctly supports product marketing campaigns and promotions.

- *VP of finance:* The vice president of finance oversees the financial viability of the sales compensation program, ensuring that its costs and benefits are consistent with company objectives.

- *Sales operations:* Sales operations provide day-to-day management of the sales compensation program. This includes plan oversight, management, and reporting.

- *Field sales management:* Field sales management provides ongoing execution and evaluation of the sales compensation program. By providing the field perspective, sales management helps assure program effectiveness and practicality.

- *Human resources:* The compensation manager provides external competitive market practices by purchasing reliable survey data. The compensation manager also examines internal equity of program fairness as compared to compensation programs provided to various nonsales jobs.

- *Legal:* The legal department approves plan documentation and program management to assure compliance with legal obligations.

- *Sales personnel:* Sales management solicits feedback from sales personnel through field interviews, focus group sessions, surveys, and one-on-one interviews with first-line sales managers.

The costly sales force. The chief financial officer (CFO) became alarmed at the increasing relative cost of sales and called for a review of compensation levels. However, on review, the pay levels proved competitive with external pay levels. *The market for test and measurement equipment is cyclical. The CFO noted that the company's cost of sales was increasing at a greater rate than competitors' cost of sales. Additional market analysis demonstrated that competitors' pay practices were more variable—less base salary and greater use of variable compensation. While not clear to the CFO, he presumed the compensation program was most likely contributing to the high cost of sales. When examined, the pay levels, regardless of pay mix, were very similar to those of sales personnel at the competitors. The CFO was correct on one account: The sales force was too costly. However, it was not the pay program. Further research showed that sales force productivity was lagging the competitors. While the quota sizes were comparative, the overall number of managerial, overlay specialists, marketing personnel, and headquarters staff was way above competitor levels. Preferred Solution: Leave the sales head count and compensation plan alone; reduce staffing everywhere else.*

Using Committees

We recommend the use of several sales compensation committees when feasible. To be effective, sales compensation plans frequently must reconcile competing objectives. A committee approach can best help raise and resolve these divergent issues. The following is an example of various types of sales compensation committees. Use them to drive best thinking, collaboration, and effectiveness of design.

- *Sales compensation design team:* We believe companies should entrust the design of the sales compensation program to a working committee represented by sales, field management, finance, marketing, and human resources. Charter this committee to examine current practices and suggest new sales compensation solutions for the next operating period.

Should Sales Representatives Sit on the Sales Compensation Design Team? *Companies report success in having sales representatives as part of the sales compensation design team. As consultants, we try to avoid this practice. Yes, we want input from the field personnel about the current program, but the leadership team needs to make company-serving decisions about changes to the sales compensation program. Putting sales representatives on such a committee may compromise them with their peers or management and might misdirect the need to take new or dissimilar actions. Finally, participating in meetings about making pay changes may be protected activities as defined by the National Labor Relations Act so companies should check with their lawyers first before inviting a sales representative to sit on their design team.*

- *Sales compensation leadership committee:* Many business units have a management committee comprised of sales, marketing, operations, and finance leaders. This leadership committee can specify the company's sales compensation design principles, reconfirm the business objectives, and approve plans as drafted by the sales compensation design team.
- *Sales compensation program management committee:* The program management committee has an ongoing responsibility for

providing oversight to the sales compensation program application and interpretation. Meeting once a quarter, this committee can review and make decisions on program adjustments, plan exceptions, and policy interpretations. Additionally, this committee can provide ongoing program reviews by evaluating assessment reports prepared by sales operations and finance. It is a prudent exercise to completely document all decisions.

- *Sales compensation administration team:* For some organizations, program administration is significant, requiring continual oversight and management. In larger organizations, the administration of the sales compensation program might be shared by various parties such as sales operations, finance, commission accounting, payroll, and IT. Companies should bring these responsible parties together into a committee to make sure administration issues are resolved quickly, checks are issued in a timely manner, and real-time reports are available to management and sales personnel.

Sales Compensation—The Process Manager

Appoint a process manager to oversee the whole sales compensation program including alignment, design, management, administration, assessment, audit, and legal. The process manager might report to sales and be found in the sales operations department. However, it's not uncommon for the process manager to come from another department. For example, this individual might be found in human resources, finance, or marketing. It's not important where the person sits; the most important thing is that he or she has the skills to manage all the complex issues related to sales compensation design. No one should presume that this position is the sales compensation czar. Instead, the appointed person should manage the process of sales compensation program design, management, and administration. The sales compensation process manager will set dates, confirm accountabilities, and oversee the application of the program. This person should never be tasked with the objective to design new plans. Assign this duty to the sales compensation design team and let the process manager manage the process.

Summary

Effective sales compensation design is an inclusive process involving key stakeholders: the general manager, vice president of marketing, vice president of sales, and vice president of finance. Staff specialists contribute to the effort by conducting fact finding, analyzing the current plan, gathering external market data, and managing the design process.

4

Why Job Content Drives Sales Compensation Design

As we mentioned earlier, sales compensation is driven by sales job content. While industry practices, motivation theory, and company philosophy play contributing roles, the design of a sales compensation plan reflects the type of sales job it supports. In this chapter, we will examine why job content drives sales compensation design. We will look at how different job components combine to form different sales job types. We will then present an inventory of sales jobs. Next, we will look at sales job design errors and how they have a negative impact on sales compensation plan effectiveness. Finally, we will provide examples of sales jobs and their supporting sales compensation elements.

Job Content Drives Sales Compensation Design

Sales compensation is a contributing reason why salespeople want to excel. However, in our view, it is seldom the *primary* reason. Human endeavor is a complex chemistry of intrinsic and extrinsic needs. Leadership models, measurement systems, affiliation variables, and supporting programs (such as the rewards system) contribute to provide the proper direction and motivation to the sales force. Our experience with hundreds of sales forces suggests that beginning with sales job content is a rational and safe starting point for effective sales compensation design. We don't want to preclude alternative approaches or theories. In our view, other variables can explain the existence of unique sales compensation designs but job content can best explain the construct of most sales compensation plans. Perhaps a storyboard will help illustrate how sales compensation design logically flows from job content:

> "Okay, Ms. Smith," begins the sales manager. "We have an excellent sales territory for you. You will be calling on small businesses in

three zip codes. Your job is to sell telecommunication services to customers already using the major carrier in the market. It's not an easy sell, but we have a great product, superior customer service, and great pricing. Expect a lot of 'Nos' but don't give up! Now, let me give you an idea of how your compensation package will work. You will receive a commission on all new accounts. You will get a percentage of the revenue for the first 6 months of any new account. After that, the customer will be handled by the customer service team. Although your base salary is low, you have a great upside earning opportunity tied to your sales success."

As this storyboard illustrates, it is almost impossible to split the job content (new account selling) from its supporting sales compensation program (commission on all new sales).

Although most people can list 10 to 15 different types of sales jobs, the list actually totals close to 50 distinct selling jobs. Not all industries or companies use all 50 sales jobs. In fact, it's unlikely that a sales department will use more than 15 or 20 sales jobs and will more likely need only 8 to 12 sales jobs. As we will demonstrate, the foundation of sales compensation design rests with the underlying job content—regardless of the industry or company.

Sales Job Components

In Chapter 1, we presented Sales Process: Demand Creation, Buyer Identification, Purchase Commitment, Order Fulfillment, and Customer Service. Sales organizations need to be "outward facing," supporting different customer populations. In this section, we add two more variables that help further define job content: Customer Segments and Customer Specialization.

- *Customer Segments:* Customer segments include the following categories:
  - *New accounts:* New accounts are prospects that are not current buyers. More narrowly defined segments may identify multiple unique buyers within an account, thus increasing the population of "new" accounts.
  - *Existing accounts:* Existing accounts are current buyers. A company's definition of "former customers" will help correctly assign these returning customers to the right category: "new" or "existing."

- *Channel partners:* Channel partners represent a vast number of different types of partners who sell products on behalf of the company. Examples include retailers, distributors, value-added resellers, dealers, brokers, agents, and manufacturing representatives. Companies that rely on channel partners deploy indirect sales representatives known as channel representatives to support the channel partners, providing training, promoting product sales, and resolving partner-customer service issues.
- *Channel end users:* In some cases, the manufacturer will deploy influencing personnel to call on end-user customers. They create demand for the product and help identify buyers but refer the customer to the channel partner for purchase execution and order fulfillment.

- *Customer Specialization:* Customer specialization includes four major groups of customers:
  - *Stratified:* One of the more popular methods used to group customers is by size. This approach presumes that larger customers have needs different from smaller customers.
  - *Product/Application:* Another method by which to group customers, for sales coverage purposes, is by product or application. In this approach, sales personnel sell a uniform family of products or applications.
  - *Industry:* Certain industries may require specialized sellers knowledgeable about industry issues to properly represent their companies' services.
  - *Geographic:* A final and practical method for specializing customers is by geographic location.

An example of how these various components (process, segments, and specialization) configure into a job can be seen in Figure 4-1. The shading reflects the role of a new account sales representative like Ms. Smith from our storyboard.

Figure 4-2 shows the role of a major account sales representative.

Figure 4-3 shows sales channel representatives with both channel partner and end-user responsibilities. The sales channel representative sells to the channel partners and promotes purchases to end users, but sales channel representatives do not write end-user orders. In such cases, he or she refers the order to one of the channel partners.

Customer Variables		Sales Process				
Segment	Specialization	Demand Creation	Buyer Identification	Purchase Commitment	Order Fulfillment	Customer Service
New Accounts	Stratified					
	Product					
	Industry					
	Geographic	X	X	X	X	
Existing Accounts	Stratified					
	Product					
	Industry					
	Geographic					
Channel Partners	Stratified					
	Product					
	Industry					
	Geographic					
Channel End Users	Stratified					
	Product					
	Industry					
	Geographic					

Figure 4-1. New Account Sales Representative

Customer Variables		Sales Process				
Segment	Specialization	Demand Creation	Buyer Identification	Purchase Commitment	Order Fulfillment	Customer Service
New Accounts	Stratified	X	X	X	X	X
	Product					
	Industry					
	Geographic					
Existing Accounts	Stratified		X	X	X	X
	Product					
	Industry					
	Geographic					
Channel Partners	Stratified					
	Product					
	Industry					
	Geographic					
Channel End Users	Stratified					
	Product					
	Industry					
	Geographic					

Figure 4-2. Major Account Sales Representative

Customer Variables		Sales Process				
Segment	Specialization	Demand Creation	Buyer Identification	Purchase Commitment	Order Fulfillment	Customer Service
New Accounts	Stratified					
	Product					
	Industry					
	Geographic					
Existing Accounts	Stratified					
	Product					
	Industry					
	Geographic					
Channel Partners	Stratified					
	Product	X	X	X		
	Industry					
	Geographic					
Channel End Users	Stratified					
	Product	X	X			
	Industry					
	Geographic					

Figure 4-3. Sales Channel Representative

Figures 4-1 to 4-3 show just how sales process, customer segments, customer specialization, and sales process steps configure into unique sales jobs.

Sales Job Type Inventory

The following sales job inventory presents a comprehensive list of sales job types. We have grouped sales jobs into six job families:

1. *Income producers:* Income producers define their value as having specialized customer access and typically sell nondifferentiated products.

2. *Direct sales jobs:* Direct sales jobs sell to end users and act as the primary contact to the customer. Direct sellers work either outside the company or are telephone sales personnel. Sales personnel can work for the manufacturer or for a sales channel member such as a distributor, dealer, retailer, or broker.

3. *Indirect sales jobs:* Indirect sales jobs work with partners and other third-party representatives who sell the product on behalf of the manufacturer or service creator.

4. *Overlay sales jobs:* Overlay sales jobs work with, and in support of, the account sales force. They provide additional help to the sales representative.

5. *Business development:* Business development jobs promote and develop market access.

6. *Pre- and postsales support:* These are technical personnel who assist during pre- and/or postsales efforts.

We present the list of jobs for each sales job family next.

Income Producers

Income producers sell other companies' products. However, for the income producer, their true asset is their own loyal customer base.

Agent/Broker/Producer	Agents, brokers, and producers are normally dedicated to a single employer. The employers of agents, brokers, and producers do not make products, nor do they purchase (take possession of) the products they sell.
Independent rep	Independent reps are similar to agents, brokers, and producers but are not dedicated to a single employer and may represent noncompetitive products from various manufacturers.
Investment manager	Investment managers provide financial planning advice to investors earning commission income for the sale of investment vehicles.
Multi-tier marketing rep	Multi-tier marketing reps sell products and services directly to consumers. Examples include Avon and Amway.
Property development specialist	Property development specialists help arrange real estate investments with payouts occurring before and,

	sometimes, after distribution or syndication of the investment.
Trader	Traders buy and sell products and earn income by sharing a percentage of the difference between the buy price and the sell price.

Direct Sales Jobs

Direct sales jobs sell to the end user. The company may be the manufacturer or reseller of the product.

Asset manager	Sells to and collaborates with high-revenue customers on a national or worldwide basis May have access to local (remote location) sales resources
Channel assignment seller	Advises customers as to the most effective channel to meet their needs Matriculates the customer in the channel (e.g., convinces customers to use the Web as the preferred purchase channel)
Customer service/Order representative	Accepts inbound calls and books customer orders No cross-selling or up-selling
Dealer (showroom)	Sells to customers from showroom floor that presents product for ordering
Event/Project seller	Sells a major project to a customer No ongoing account responsibility
Geographic	Sells to assigned accounts within a geographic area Calls on existing and new customers
Geographic— New accounts	Sells to new accounts only within a geographic territory

Global account	Sells to existing, named, large customers on a worldwide basis Does not have local sales resources reports
Government	Sells to tax-supported entities such as government or military units
Major account	Sells to a select list of large-named accounts
Major account (existing)	Sells to a select list of existing, large accounts
Major account (new)	Sells to a select list of potential, major accounts who are now noncustomers
Market maker	Sells a new product to noncustomers—creates market for product
Named account	Sells to an identified list of accounts
National account	Sells to the headquarters of a major, named customer to secure vendor approval for local selling efforts by others
Product (product, service, application)	Sells a specific product/service or application within a territory or to assigned accounts Sole owner of the buyer/account
Referral sales	Sells to new customers via referrals from existing customers No assigned territory, a.k.a. "daisy chain selling"
Renewal	Sells to existing customers' renewal of an existing contract
Store sales (floor)—retail	Sells from existing floor inventory product (retail)
Telephone account representative	Sells product and services to preidentified accounts—both inbound and outbound sales efforts
Telephone sales representative	Sells products and services to nonassigned accounts—both inbound and outbound

Telesales—Outbound	Sells products and services to nonassigned accounts on an outbound basis only
Telesales—Inbound	Up-sells and cross-sells on inbound sales opportunities
Telesales—Renewal	Outbound calls to customers with expiring contracts for contract renewal purposes May call on former customers to reestablish contract/service (win back sellers)
Vertical/Industry	Sells to a specific vertical or industrial market
Win back	Sells to former customers to win back the departed customer

The cost of overselling customers. The state Public Utilities Commission (PUC) fined a major telecommunication company millions of dollars for unethical selling practices. Was the incentive plan the cause? *Service representatives at phone companies handle customer requests for new phone service, change in service, and billing issues. The state PUC sets billing rates to ensure the phone company offers quality service levels. Telephone companies can earn additional income by selling enhanced services to customers such as call waiting, an extra line, call forwarding, and long-distance services. U.S. border states are popular entry points for recent immigrants. When calling for new phone service, these new immigrants—identified by their accented English—were targeted for packaged solutions loaded with enhanced features at a higher cost. They were not offered the much lower-priced basic service. The PUC identified the incentive plan as the culprit. However, when examined, the incentive could only partially explain the motivation behind this type of predatory selling. The upside earning potential was only 5 percent of base salary, an amount too modest to explain widespread overselling. On further investigation, the source of pressure to oversell customers was not the incentive plan, but supervisors' insistence on hitting the numbers. The supervisors were under significant pressure to grow revenues. Preferred Solution: Recharter the customer service model to meet* *customer needs first. Retrain supervisors. Use other sales channels to promote enhanced products other than overselling on inbound service calls. (Of interest, it was employees—the service representatives—who alerted the PUC about the abusive selling tactics that were being foisted on them by their supervisors.)*

Indirect Sales Jobs

Indirect sellers work with sales channel partners and other third parties who sell products to end users. Indirect sellers do not sell to end users; the channel partner is responsible for the sale.

Channel end-user representative	Works with end-user customers to promote products that are purchased from channel partners Works with assigned channel partners
Channel representative	Promotes products to channel partner, who resells products to customers Works with channel member sales personnel of channel partners such as value added resellers (VARs), retailers, distributors, brokers, and independent software vendors (ISV) May also call on end users to help promote channel partner sales
HQ sales-in (retail)	Sells products to the headquarters of retail chains
Influence seller (missionary selling)	Promotes products to influencers who can specify product purchase; examples of such purchase influencers include doctors, consultants, engineers, and architects
In-store sales-out	Works in retail outlets to place and/or promote company products Sometimes referred to as merchandisers

| Jobber | Restocks customer products at retail locations
May promote product placement |
| Original equipment manufacturer (OEM) seller | Sells products (e.g., components, subsystems) to manufacturers that incorporate into a final manufactured product |

Overlay Sales Jobs

Overlay sales jobs work in support of direct sales jobs and, occasionally, indirect sales jobs to provide additional sales support to the primary seller.

Application specialist	An application specialist has an in-depth knowledge of a specific application or family of applications Assists the assigned seller to help promote the application to customers or channel partners
Product specialist	A product specialist has an in-depth knowledge of a select product or family of products Assists the assigned seller to help promote the product to customers or channel partners
Service specialist	A service specialist has an in-depth knowledge of a select service or family of services Assists the assigned seller to help promote the service to the customer or channel partner
Vertical specialist	A vertical specialist has an in-depth knowledge of a specific industry or buyer type Assists assigned sellers to help promote the company's products or services to a specific vertical/industry market

Business Development

A business development resource promotes the company's products and services to emerging market opportunities with customers or channel partners. These individuals usually do not have sales goals but are given management by objective (MBO)–type measures.

Alliance/Joint venture specialist	Establishes company's alliance and joint venture partnership efforts May or may not manage ongoing relationship
Channel end-user representative	End-user channel representative calls on end users to stimulate product sales but refers sales opportunities to sanctioned channel partners Not dedicated to support any channel partner
New channel developer	Recruits new channel partners
New offering specialist	New offering specialist presents the company's product and service to customers to test customer interest, confirm the value proposition, and identify the preferred market segments

Pre- and Post-Sales Support

Pre- and post-sales technical support are not considered sales personnel but are often an integral part of the selling effort. They have customer contact and frequently influence the customer to act; however, a direct or indirect salesperson owns the account and the pre- and post-sales support person works at the salesperson's direction.

Post-sales technical support	Works with sales personnel to help install, adopt, and implement the purchased solution
Pre- and post-sales technical support	Works with sales personnel on both pre- and post-sales technical issues

| Pre-sales technical support | Works with sales personnel to facilitate the sales to customers |
| | Provides technical support including interpretation, need requirements, and solution configuration |

The above job inventory presents over 50 different sales jobs. We assume there are more jobs than this. However, these are the most prevalent and represent over 90 percent of all sellers. Each company may provide a unique name for the job but regardless of the title, most jobs can be matched based on their content to one of the job types listed above.

Job Levels

Job levels reflect the gradation of impact, experience, and defined importance of the job. The higher the level, the greater the expected output of the incumbent and, correspondingly, the greater the target total cash compensation for a job. Progression from one job level to the next is a reward for individual performance. Level titles vary significantly from industry to industry and company to company. For example, the title of vice president might be given to high-level sales personnel in the banking industry whereas a similar job might be called a sales executive in a high-technology company. Normally, job levels can be broken down into four generic levels:

1. *Associate:* A common title for an entry-level sales job is sales associate. It denotes the lowest job level on the organization chart.

2. *Representative:* A sales representative is a fully trained salesperson accountable for his or her actions and assigned responsibilities.

3. *Senior representative:* A senior sales representative is a seasoned sales representative. He or she will most likely have the same job content as a sales representative but will have proved him- or herself with demonstrated, sustained, productive performance over a period of time. Often given more autonomy than a representative, this position usually has the highest head count in a well-configured sales department.

4. *Account executive:* An account executive is the most senior sales level requiring advanced selling and customer skills. The account executive may act as an individual seller or coordinate (lead) the efforts of other sellers too.

Each of the 50-plus jobs listed above could, conceivably, have all four job levels, thus increasing the number of distinct sales and sales-like jobs to over 200.

Job Design Errors

As mentioned ealier, sales compensation follows job design. One of the challenges facing sales strategists is to design and deploy effective sales jobs. An effective sales job has focus, clarity of purpose, and a clearly identified point of persuasion responsibility. While the point of persuasion should be the primary focus, sometimes multiple constraints often (and sometimes, correctly) compromise this singular focus.

- *Costs:* Although we would like to have sales personnel focus all their time on selling activities and let others do the customer service work, the cost to hire others to perform such nonselling tasks may not be plausible. Therefore, the salesperson may find that other customer-related tasks will displace selling time.

- *Customer expectations:* An unhappy customer is not inclined to make additional purchases from a salesperson. Therefore, the salesperson must shift from selling activities to customer service responsibilities in order to improve the customer's current satisfaction before returning to pure selling efforts.

- *Product or service configuration:* Sometimes the product or service configuration precludes exclusive focus on selling. For example, in some services, the seller is expected to also deliver the solution as in the case of custom training or consulting.

However, the best sales forces will continually adjust sales job content to ensure that focus of the job is at the point of persuasion. The following is a list of the four most common sales job design errors:

- *Sales Job Design Error 1: The Corrupted Sales:* Sometimes referred to as a contaminated sales job. Responsibilities of other departments have crept into the selling job, such as collections, marketing, and customer service.

- *Sales Job Design Error 2: The Blended Sales Job:* Sales jobs function best when they have a single focus. Focus occurs when the goals are few and the cadence is uniform. Too many goals overwhelm the focus of a sales job. This can occur when the seller is given several selling tasks to undertake at one time: "Sell new business, sell to existing customers, and work with channel partners." Each of these tasks is vital and warranted but when combined into the same job, the result is a blended job with too many goals. Blended sales jobs can also erode sales cadence—the rhythm of activity. Selling to the major customer has a long cycle while selling to new, smaller customers may have a very short sales cycle. In this case, the cadences of the two sales jobs are at odds with each other, contributing to the blended job design error.

- *Sales Job Design Error 3: Bandwidth Exceeded:* Another job design error begins with good intentions but often produces a third error in job design: too many products and too many dissimilar customers for the salesperson to handle. Today's electronic sales support has given sales forces more bandwidth but there is a limit to the breadth of products and customers that a salesperson can manage. Overloading a sales job will cause the incumbents to start ignoring elements of the product and customer mix.

- *Sales Job Design Error 4: Undetected Job Transformation:* Although not a true job design error, some jobs transform from an initial job to a new, different job. Same person, same sales territory, and same accounts, but the first job (open new accounts) transforms upon success into a second job (manage the base of business). While this is a preferred business outcome, sometimes the measurement and reward systems do not transform at the same time to match the new, evolved job. The result is a misalignment between job content selling tactics.

Sales management needs to rectify sales job design errors prior to drafting sales compensation plans.

Job Type	Title	Mix and Leverage	Measures
Income Producers	Agent	N/A	Commission on all sales
	Independent Rep	N/A	Commission on all sales
Direct Sales Representatives	Asset Manager	80/20, 2.5x	Return on Sales
	Geographic Rep	60/40, 3.5x	All Sales
	Major Account Rep	75/25, 3x	Sales & Retention
	Telesales Inbound	80/20, 3x	Up-sell, Cross-sell
	Telesales Outbound	50/50, 3x	New Sales
	Vertical Rep	70/30, 3x	Vertical Sales
Indirect Sales Representatives	Channel Rep	75/25, 3x	Sales & Channel Balance
	OEM Seller	70/30, 3x	New Placements
Overlay Specialist	Application Specialist	80/20, 2.5x	Sales & New Accounts
	Product Specialist	80/20, 2.5x	Sales & Rep Balance
Business Development	Alliance Specialist	100/0 +25%	New Alliances MBO
	Channel End User	90/10, 2.5x	Sell Through
Technical Support	Presales Tech Support	90/10, 2.5x	District Sales
	Postsales Tech Support	100/0 +10%	District Sales

Figure 4-4. Job Type and Pay Plan Design

Sales Compensation Practices by Job Types

Figure 4-4 provides examples of different pay mixes, leverages, and measures by job type. These are sample illustrations of how sales job content affects pay plans.

Summary

Our experience has shown that when sales compensation plans become ineffective, it is usually because the plans attempt to fix a job design mistake. In particular, be on the lookout for corrupted and blended sales jobs. A sales compensation project always examines job content for clarity and focus.

5

Formula Types

At the core of every sales compensation plan is a formula that translates sales performance into income for the salesperson. This chapter presents a comprehensive listing of the different types of sales compensation formulas. All of these formulas are effective within a proper context. In other words, they are neither good nor bad, but can be effective or ineffective depending on their application. We offer observations about each formula for your consideration.

Illustrating Formula Payouts with Sales Compensation Formula Graphs

To facilitate our presentation of the incentive compensation formula types, we will use a popular convention for presenting sales compensation designs: the sales compensation formula graph. The sales compensation formula graph provides a visual representation of the pay formula. We will be able to present many different types of plans on the formula graph. The basic construction of the formula graph is shown in Figure 5-1.

Note: Compensation (pay) is always displayed on the vertical (y axis) and sales performance is displayed on the horizontal (x axis) in Figure 5-1.

Figure 5-2 provides notations with callouts printed on the formula graph. The two callouts show the 1st and 2nd commission rates. From a mathematical perspective, the commission rate is the slope, or the relationship between compensation and performance.

Two Major Seller Categories

As described earlier, there are two major categories of sales jobs: *income producers* and *sales representatives*. The underlying economic

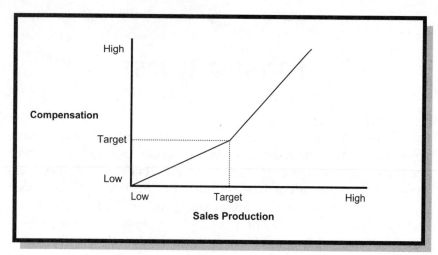

Figure 5-1. Compensation Formula Graph

foundation differs from one to the other. Income producers share a percent of the revenue, whereas sales representatives earn incentive payments as a portion of a predetermined target earnings amount. While both seller categories share many of the same mathematical formula mechanics, the basis of pay is profoundly different. Income producers have shared ownership of the sales results, regardless of earn-

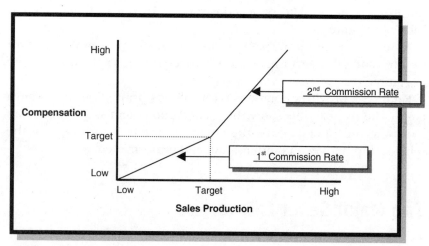

Figure 5-2. Compensation Formula Graph

ing level, either low or high. Conversely, sales representatives earn a portion of a target incentive amount. In this respect, the company's commitment and obligation are to the target earning opportunity and not to a percent of the revenue. For sales representatives, management determines what level of performance warrants what level of incentive pay.

Seller Category: Income Producers

In this section, we will examine the pay practices for income producers.

We would expect the pay mechanics for income producers to be relatively easy to present. In concept, income producer pay programs are based on a simple premise: Income producers are "the business" and they receive a share or portion of every sale. As a result, the pay plan should be an easy-to-understand straight commission expressed as a percent of sales production dollars. However, many variations of income producer pay plans exist.

Income Producer Plans

We present the following income producer plan types:

1. Flat commission
2. Ramped commission
3. Residuals/Trailing/Back-end payouts
4. Pools
5. Multi-tier marketing

Income Producer Plan 1: Flat Commission

The flat commission schedule (see Figure 5-3) is the simplest of all sales compensation formulas. The formula is stated as a percent of sales dollar production or fixed payment for each unit sold. Here are examples of flat commission plans:

Example 1: 6% commission paid for all sales dollars

Example 2: 25% commission paid on all gross margin dollars

Example 3: $10 commission paid for each unit sold

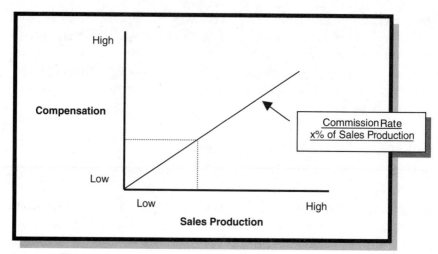

Figure 5-3. Income Producer 1: Flat Commission

Note: In the example in Figure 5-3, the payment begins with the first dollar or unit of sale. So, there is no threshold that must be reached before payments can begin, nor is there a cap or maximum payment either. In this illustration, commission earnings are unlimited.

Observations

A flat commission, with no base salary, is a very powerful and focused pay program. Expect the income producer sales force to look primarily to the pay program for direction and focus.

Vocabulary Alert: Flat commission and straight commission are different. The term *flat commission* means a constant or unchanging rate. Straight commission represents a different concept. The term *straight commission* means no base salary, with all earnings achieved through the sales compensation program. The following sentence correctly illustrates this usage: The compensation program features a straight commission with no base salary; the flat commission formula pays the same rate on all sales production.

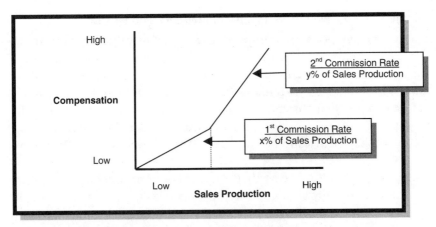

Figure 5-4. Income Producer 2: Ramped Commission—Progressive

Income Producer Plan 2: Ramped Commission

While the flat commission formula does not change, a ramped commission schedule has more than one commission rate. If the second commission rate is higher than the first, then the ramp is known as a progressive ramp. Progressive ramps are also known as accelerators.

In Figure 5-4, we see that the commission rate increases after some level of accomplishment is achieved, in this case, $1 million. The commission formula for a ramped commission schedule is shown in Figure 5-5.

Observations

A progressive ramp commission formula improves the motivation of a flat commission plan. Use this approach when more sales are difficult, but very desirable to the company.

Component	Progressive Ramp Commission Schedule		
		Sales Performance	Commission Rate
Commission Rate	1st Commission Rate 2nd Commission Rate	To $1M $1M and Over	6% 8%

Figure 5-5. Progressive Ramp Commission Schedule

Income Producer Plan 3: Residuals/Trailing/Back-End Payouts

For certain types of income producers, the full value of the transaction is not realized at the time of sale. There are different examples of this occurrence. For example, in some cases, revenue continues on an annual basis such as with life insurance premiums. Figure 5-6 is an example of a residual commission schedule used by the life insurance industry. The value of the recurring revenue has value on a declining basis, eventually providing no income to the salesperson by the fourth year.

Because the seller is classified as an income producer, these future earnings are usually assured unless abridged by the payment policy. In some instances, there is a buyout provision to make payments on these future earnings if the income producer should leave prior to realization of these earnings. Trailing is another expression for residuals.

In other cases, the final value of the transaction is not fully recognized until the disposition of an investment. Companies configure numerous back-end payouts depending on their unique circumstances. Back-end payouts are common in property and real estate development when the true value of the deal is not realized until the investment and/or property is sold at some future date. As specified in contract language, the income producer will earn a percent of profits (normally) when the investment is sold, syndicated, liquidated, or transferred.

Observations

Paying for future revenue or profits is the annuity element of income producer plans.

Component	Residual Commission Schedule	
Commission Rate	**Insurance Premium Residuals**	
	Portion of	
	Year of Policy	Annual Premium
	1	100%
	2	75%
	3	25%
	4	0%

Figure 5-6. Residual Commission Schedule

Income Producer Plan 4: Pools

Use pool payments when a group of income producers work together to realize shared income. Some traders (currency, bond, electrical power, and many others) often work on a trading desk as part of a team.

A pool accumulates the earnings of the transactions executed by the income producers. This block of money is then distributed at the end of each performance period by a predefined formula or methodology as illustrated in Figure 5-7.

Some organizations use a hybrid individual and pool model. One hybrid approach features a commission paid to individuals for normal transactions and the earnings for mega deals partially allocated to a pool for distribution at the end of the performance period. Another hybrid approach is to accumulate the pool based on performance, but allow manager judgment of individual contribution to affect some or all of the pool payout to participants.

Observations

Pools are not widely used except for certain trading and financial markets. Pools are not effective at driving (causing) team performance. They are primarily a mechanism for sharing results.

> **Vocabulary Alert:** *Participation rate* is a term often used for income producers to define their share of the income. While this is the same idea as a commission rate, the implicit sense of ownership is reaffirmed by the use of the phrase *participation rate,* implying a shared ownership in the results—a concept consistent with incentive compensation plans for income producers.

Component	Traders' Pool	
Traders' Pool	25% of all trading earnings are accumulated in the Traders' Pool	
	Title	Portion of Traders' Pool
	Sr. Traders	50%—divided equally
	Traders	35%—divided equally
	Trading Assistants	15%—divided equally

Figure 5-7. Traders' Pool

Income Producer Plan 5: Multi-Tier Marketing

Multi-tier marketing uses the concepts of overrides and pyramids in a correct and positive fashion. Each person gets paid a commission on sales. The real money is found in recruiting a distribution network (pyramid) of people who sell products for which an override is paid. The more sellers recruited, the more money earned through override payments.

An override provides proportional payment to the supervisor. With large distribution networks, several layers of sellers, supervisors, and managers make payments from one level up to the next level.

Observations

Multi-tier marketers generally promote high energy and positive thinking but normally absorb high turnover. Normally, several individuals have the potential to earn substantial income by building effective distribution and/or recruitment networks. Seller costs are fully variable but long-term commitment is fleeting.

Seller Category: Sales Representatives

In this section, we will examine numerous incentive formulas used for sales representatives.

Without close examination, it's easy to misclassify a sales representative as an income producer, and, therefore, provide an inappropriate pay program. We estimate that sales representatives account for over 90 percent of all sellers, while the remaining 10 percent are income producers. Again, here's a brief definition of the two categories of sellers:

- *Income producers:* Income producers are sellers who control (own) their accounts. The product they sell is usually a commodity and is, therefore, undifferentiated. The value of the business is the contacts and relationships of the seller with his or her customers. Normally, an income producer arrives with a "book of business" and if he or she departs, he or she takes over 80 percent of the business with them. Income producers are paid a percent of the sales production. Funding for the incentive comes from sales results. Competitive market comparison is made by assessing percentage paid, not by actual dollars earned.

- *Sales representatives:* Sales representatives sell a unique offering of the company. The value to the customer is the company's products and services and not the salesperson. Companies manage sales representatives' pay to a target incentive amount. For performance below goal, the pay is less than the target incentive amount. For performance above goal, the incentive payment is above the target incentive amount.

Sales Representative or Marketing Representative? *Some field customer contact jobs appear to be those of sales representatives but are, in fact, marketing jobs. If the field person is executing a brand strategy such as providing product displays or training channel sales personnel without any influencing role, then the job might be a marketing job. Marketing jobs can be eligible for add-on incentives, but normally not sales compensation.*

Starting with a Target Incentive Amount

When building a compensation program for income producers, we start with a commission rate. When we build a sales compensation program for sales representatives, we begin with a target incentive amount. As an intended result, the pay of sales representatives' earnings are managed to an expected target incentive amount.

There are other significant implications when using a target incentive:

- *Earnings commitment:* For income producers, the company commits to the commission percentage. For sales representatives, the company is making a commitment to the target earnings opportunity.

- *Funding:* Funding for income producers' commissions comes from revenue production. For sales representatives, incentive compensation is cross-funded by the plan participants. For sales representatives, the target pay is reallocated among the participants with better performers making more than the target incentive pay for the job and less effective performers making less than the target incentive pay.

Calculation Engines: Commission versus Bonus

There are many formula methods for calculating the sales compensation payments for sales representatives. These formula methods fall into two major groupings: target incentive commission formula (TI-Commission) and target incentive bonus formula (TI-Bonus). In both cases, the construction of the incentive plan begins with identifying a target incentive amount. Once the target incentive amount is selected, a commission or bonus formula is identified to provide the calculation engine for the sales compensation payout. The differences between the TI-Commission and the TI-Bonus are described below.

A TI-Commission looks very much like the commission schedule used for income producers. The incentive payment is expressed as a percent of sales results or payment per unit. However, while the formula constructs look almost identical to those used for income producers, the underlying design assumptions are very different. For sales representatives, each job title is assigned a target incentive amount. Assuming that the territories are of equal potential, a commission rate is calculated to ensure that the target incentive level of pay is earned for the target level of expected performance. The formula for calculating a commission rate is as follows:

$$\frac{\text{target incentive amount}}{\text{target volume}} \times 100 = \text{commission rate}$$

Or, as an illustration:

$$\frac{\$100,000}{\$2,000,000} \times 100 = 5\% \text{ commission rate}$$

For TI-Bonus plans, earnings are expressed as a percent of target incentive earnings for performance as compared to quota. Use the TI-Bonus formula when territories are not of equal size but you wish to provide similar earnings opportunities. Whether the territory is $1M or $2M, $5M or $10M, accomplishment of sales objectives can be expressed as a percent of goal: 75 percent of goal, 100 percent of goal, or 125 percent of goal, for example. In this manner, the formula expresses payments as a percent of goal achieved and not as a percent

Component	Bonus Formula—Step-Based	
	Step-Based TI-Bonus Formula	
	Percent to Quota	**Percent of Target Incentive**
Bonus Schedule	Over 125%	150%
	110% to 124%	125%
	105% to 109%	110%
	100% to 104%	100%
	90% to 99%	75%
	80% to 89%	50%
	Below 80%	0%

Figure 5-8. Target Incentive Bonus Formula

of absolute dollars. The outcome of this approach is to provide similar earnings opportunities for dissimilar-sized territories. The TI-Bonus formula manages payouts in relation to quota, regardless of the absolute size of the territories. Figure 5-8 presents an example of the TI-Bonus formula.

In this case, the TI-Bonus formula makes payouts regardless of actual size of the territory. For example, 100 percent of quota can differ by employee, but the target incentive remains the same, thus equalizing the earning opportunities among territories.

Employee	Territory Actual dollar	Percent quota	Target incentive
A	$1.5M	100%	$35,000
B	$1.75M	100%	$35,000
C	$1.25M	100%	$35,000
D	$3.0M	100%	$35,000
E	$2.58M	100%	$35,000

In summary, use the TI-Commission formula when sales territories have similar revenue opportunities. When sales territories do not have equal revenue potential, then use the TI-Bonus formula. In Chapter 6, we will learn how to calculate commission (and bonus) schedules.

Sales Representative Sample Plans

The following are sales representative TI-Commission sample plan designs:

1. Flat Commission

2A. Ramped Commission—Progressive

2B. Ramped Commission—Regressive

2C. Ramped Commission—Hybrid

3A. Commission Plan with Base Salary

3B. Base Salary, Threshold, and Cap

4A. Variable Rate Plan

4B. Variable Table

4C. Point Schedule Variable Commission Plan

5A. Link Commission—Hurdle

5B. Link Commission—Multiplier

5C. Link Commission—Matrix

6A. Individual Commission Rates (ICRs)

6B. Stratified Commission Rates

Sales Representative TI-Commission:
1. Flat Commission

As presented for the income producer, the flat commission schedule (see Figure 5-9) is the simplest sales compensation formula. However, you must remember that the basis for the commission rate is a function of the target incentive divided by the target sales production.

There is no threshold and no cap. This formula type assumes that territories have relatively equal potential. Often sales management will realign territories or accounts to balance the potential. Use of a TI-Commission becomes less plausible when the difference between the smallest territory and the largest territory becomes greater by a factor of 2x.

Figure 5-10 is an illustration of a TI-Commission formula (flat commission).

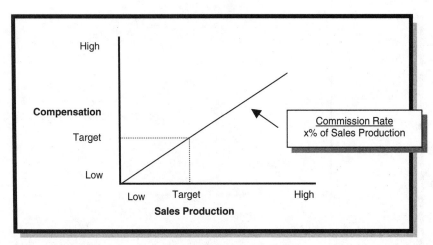

Figure 5-9. Sales Rep: 1. Flat Commission

Component	Flat Commission Schedule		
Commission Rate	Commission Rate	Sales Performance All Sales	Commission Rate 7%

Figure 5-10. Target Incentive Commission Formula (Flat Commission)

Observations

Straight commission plans (no base salary) are not common for sales representatives, although sales management might use such a plan for a high influence sales job where turnover is acceptable and full variable costs are needed.

Sales Representative TI-Commission: 2A. Ramped Commission–Progressive

Progressive ramp commission rates (see Figure 5-11) provide added motivation for selling beyond target. In a progressive ramp, the second rate is higher than the first rate. The new rate is only effective when the target amount is reached and does not (should not) "retro-back" to pay the previous sales volume at the new, higher rate.

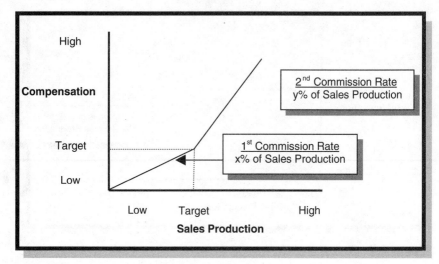

Figure 5-11. Sales Rep: 2A. Ramped Commission—Progressive

Figure 5-12 is an illustration of a ramped commission schedule. In this example, we see that the commission rate increases from 6 to 8 percent. A predetermined level of accomplishment is achieved—in this case $1.5M.

Component	Progressive Ramp Commission Schedule		
		Sales Performance	Commission Rate
Commission Rate	1st Commission Rate	To $1.5M	6%
	2nd Commission Rate	Over $1.5M	8%

Figure 5-12. Progressive Ramp Commission Schedule

Observations
Most incentive formulas feature a progressive ramp. This approach rewards additional sales performance.

Sales Representative TI-Commission: 2B. Ramped Commission—Regressive

In some instances, the commission rate declines at a predetermined level. Sales representatives do not view regressive rates favorably. However, in some instances the company needs to avoid excessive

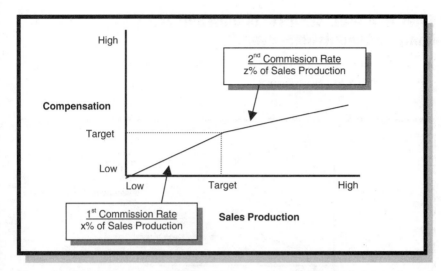

Figure 5-13. Sales Rep: 2B. Ramped Commission—Regressive

upside payments caused by either poor quota setting or unexpected windfalls. Figure 5-13, a regressive ramp rate (a lower commission rate than the first rate) serves this objective.

Figure 5-14 is an illustration of a regressive ramp commission Schedule. In this example, we see that the commission rate decreases from 7 to 5 percent. A predetermined level of accomplishment is achieved—in this case $1M.

Component	Regressive Ramp Commission Schedule		
		Sales Performance	Commission Rate
Commission Rate	1st Commission Rate	To $2.0M	7%
	2nd Commission Rate	Over $2.0M	5%

Figure 5-14. Regressive Ramp Commission Schedule

Observations

As with any regressive plan, not paying more for additional sales seems demotivational, and from the salesperson's perspective it is. Yet, when conditions exist for exceptional earnings beyond the 3x or comparative upside market rates, then the use of a regressive formula becomes more practical. However, it does present a communication challenge to sales management.

Sales Representative TI-Commission: 2C. Ramped Commission—Hybrid

In this hybrid example (see Figure 5-15), we see the use of both progressive and regressive ramps.

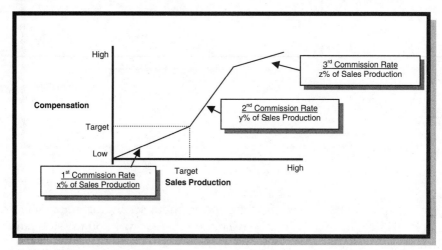

Figure 5-15. Sales Rep: 2C. Ramped Commission—Hybrid

Figure 5-16 is an illustration of a hybrid-progressive/regressive ramp commission schedule.

Component	Hybrid-Progressive/Regressive Ramp Commission Schedule		
Commission Rate	1st Commission Rate (x) 2nd Commission Rate (y) 3rd Commission Rate (z)	**Sales Performance** To $2.5M $2.5M–$5.0M Over $5.0M	**Commission Rate** 4% 7% 5%

Figure 5-16. Hybrid-Progressive/Regressive Ramp Commission Schedule

Observations

The hybrid approach uses both the positive (progressive) and negative (regressive) motivation impact of ramps. It provides additional rewards for additional sales, but after reaching a predetermined point, the commission rate declines.

Sales Representative TI-Commission: 3A.
Commission Plan with Base Salary

Straight commission plans feature pay plans with no base salary. The incentive formula provides all the earnings. Figure 5-17 illustrates commission with a base salary. The sales representative earns a commission on top of the base salary. The addition of target base salary and target incentive for the job defines the total target cash compensation assigned to the job.

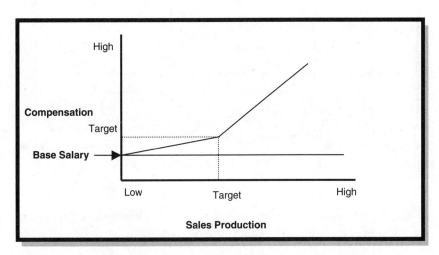

Figure 5-17. Sales Rep: 3A. Commission Plan with Base Salary

Figure 5-18 is an illustration of base salary with a progressive ramp commission schedule.

Component	Base Salary with Progressive Ramp Commission Schedule		
Part 1: Base Salary	**Base Salary/Year** **$55,000**		
Part 2: Commission Rate	1st Commission Rate 2nd Commission Rate	**Sales** **Performance** To $2.0M Over $2.0M	**Commission** **Rate** 4% 7%

Figure 5-18. Base Salary with Progressive Ramp Commission Schedule

Sales Representative TI-Commission: 3B. Base Salary, Threshold, and Cap

In Figure 5-19, we see the application of a threshold and a cap. We will learn how and when to use thresholds and caps later in this chapter.

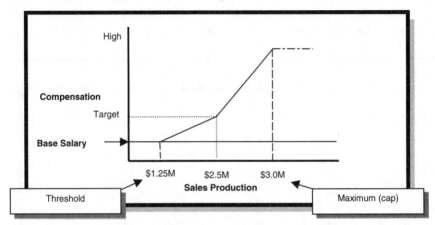

Figure 5-19. Sales Rep: 3B. Commission with Threshold, Cap, and Base Salary

Figure 5-20 is an illustration of base salary with a progressive ramp commission schedule (with threshold and maximum).

Component	Base Salary with Progressive Ramp Commission Schedule		
Part 1: Base Salary	**Base Salary/Year** **$45,000**		
Part 2: Commission Rate		**Sales Performance**	**Commission Rate**
	To Threshold	$1.25	0%
	1st Commission Rate	$1.25M–$2.5M	7%
	2nd Commission Rate	$2.5M over $3.0M	9%
	Maximum	Over $3.0M	0%

Figure 5-20. Base Salary with Progressive Ramp Commission Schedule

Observations

In addition to a base salary, this plan features a commission plan with both a threshold and a maximum. There is no payment for performance below threshold and no payment for performance above the maximum. While there are numerous reasons to use both thresholds and caps, the following are the most common:

- *Thresholds:* The primary reason for using a threshold is to avoid paying an incentive more than once for the same sale, year after year. Ongoing revenue from a previous sale should not be treated as an annuity with continuous payments made into future years. In such cases, the threshold is set at or above assured recurring revenue. There are other reasons for using a threshold. First, some organizations believe the salesperson should earn his or her base salary before an incentive is earned; therefore, the threshold is set at a number equal to the equivalent commission earnings for like sales volume. Second, some organizations want to motivate the salesperson to achieve a minimum level of quota performance. The threshold ensures that performance is consistent with this objective. Finally, other sales organizations simply use a threshold as a statement of management intent of what is the minimal level of acceptable performance.

- *Maximums:* Maximums (or caps) have always been problematic for sales organizations. Most sales forces view maximums as very demotivational. But companies use maximums for a number of reasons. The most common reason is to preclude excessive earnings for unexpected, large orders. Another reason caps are used is to offset the uncertainty of excessive payments caused by poor quota setting. Although sales management should avoid the use of maximums, their use is necessary in certain cases. Use caps when excessive sales are detrimental to the company's production capacity, or when sales personnel could achieve extraordinary sales results through unscrupulous sales practices.

Sales Representative TI-Commission: 4A. Variable Rate Plan

Variable commission plans provide different commission rates for different objectives. The most common form of variable commission plan is to provide separate commission rates for different product categories where certain products earn a high commission rate and others do not. This variation in commission rates helps guide sales representatives to the most preferred sales outcome. Figure 5-21 is an example of a variable commission plan with two different commission rates by Products A and B.

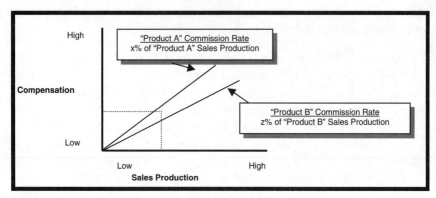

Figure 5-21. Sales Rep: 4A. Variable Rate Commission

In Figure 5-22, the two commission rates provide separate payouts depending on the product.

Component	Variable Rate Commission Schedule		
		Sales **Performance**	**Commission** **Rate**
Commission Rates	Commission Rate "x" Commission Rate "z"	Product A Product B	4% 2%

Figure 5-22. Variable Rate Commission Schedule

Observations

Variable commission rates assume that sales personnel can influence the customers' buying preference among products.

Sales Representative TI-Commission: 4B. Variable Table

The variable table (see Figure 5-23) provides another form of variable commission program. The variable commission table changes the economic value of each sales dollar prior to applying the appropriate commission rate. In this manner, the dollar value of each sale is adjusted up or down depending on the sales category. For example, a product category that has an adjustment factor of 50 percent would treat the economic value of a $100,000 sale as $50,000.

Component	Variable Table Commission Schedule		
Product Table	Adjustment to sales dollars: Product ABC — Adjustment Factor: 50% Product Blue — 110% Product Red — 90% All New Account Sales — 125% Commission rates applied to summation of the adjusted sales dollars.		
Commission Rates		Performance To Goal	Commission Rate
	1st Commission Rate	To 100%	6%
	2nd Commission Rate	Above 100%	8%

Figure 5-23. Variable Table Commission Schedule

Observations

This approach, popular with product managers, allows for the frequent fine-tuning of the sales compensation program to achieve strategic objectives. Management can make adjustments to the table values from one performance period to another.

Sales Representative TI-Commission: 4C. Point Schedule Variable Commission Plan

Another variable adjustment method is the point schedule (see Figure 5-24). Again, like other variable adjustment methods, the point schedule changes the economic value of each sale by awarding points

Component	Variable Table Commission Schedule		
Point Schedule	Points awarded for each dollar sold: Premium Products — Points/Dollar: 15 Deluxe Products — 10 Standard Products — 5 Distributed Products — 3		
Conversion Rates	Summation of points times conversion rate. Each point equals:		
		Performance To Goal	Conversion Rate
	1st Conversion Rate	To 100%	25 Cents/pt
	2nd Conversion Rate	Above 100%	35 Cents/pt

Figure 5-24. Point Schedule

depending on strategic intent. The accumulated points are then converted into dollars.

Observations

All variable adjustment methods share the same strengths and weaknesses. On the positive side, they allow the weighting of key products or sales objectives. This provides a means for management to focus efforts. It allows sales force discretion to sell what the customer needs, yet helps promote products that are strategically important to the company. The negative side of such systems is as follows:

- Such programs require a separate revenue recognition accounting system, different than the real dollars the company earns.

- There is a tendency by sales personnel to "shop the plan" or look for the right combination of market needs and their own sales proficiency. This may or may not meet the company's needs. Too many choices tend to dilute the directional impact of value adjustment programs.

About Link Designs

Link designs are one of the most advanced formula techniques available. Sometimes known as *linkages,* they tie incentive payouts to performance on two or more measures. These linkages are not simply additive—as in the more you earn on any measure the more you make. Instead, linkages provide both a positive impact on the upside of performance and a negative impact on the downside of performance.

There are three types of link formulas:

- *Hurdles:* As with all linkages, hurdles link two or more measures. A hurdle requires the salesperson to accomplish measure A before realizing the beneficial payout related to measure B. For example, no commission will be paid on product A unless the sales performance for product B exceeds 50 percent of goal.

- *Multipliers:* Multipliers tie measures together in a mathematical formula. The incentive value of the first measure is either increased or decreased depending on the performance of the second measure.

In this manner, the seller knows that the economic gain of the first measure can be altered by performance on the second measure. For example, the commission earnings from the core product will be increased or decreased based on the percent to quota sales performance on the second measure.

- *Matrices:* A matrix is another form of a link design. In a matrix, two measures are featured on a grid of rows and columns. The better the performer performs on both measures, the better the reward.

Linkages reward balanced sales efforts by rewarding the salesperson for achieving all sales objectives.

Sales Representative TI-Commission: 5A. Link Commission—Hurdle

A sales compensation plan with a hurdle provides differentiated payouts for a first measure depending on how well the seller performs on a second measure (see Figure 5-25).

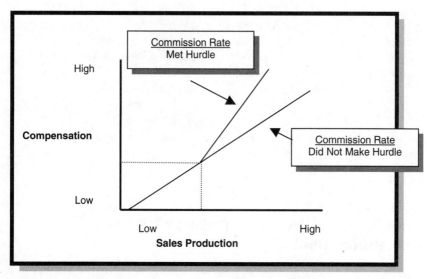

Figure 5-25. Sales Rep: 5A. Link Commission—Hurdle

Figure 5-26 illustrates a commission rate featuring a hurdle.

Component	Link Commission—Hurdle		
Commission Rate	Hurdle: Sales of Product XYZ must be at 80% of quota or higher for all revenue to receive accelerated commission earning.		
		Hurdle Performance	
		Below Hurdle	At or Above Hurdle
	Commission Rate	4%	6%
	If hurdle is not met, the below hurdle commission rate of 4% is earned.		

Figure 5-26. Link Commission with Hurdle

Observations

A hurdle provides focus to sales efforts. Outstanding performance without meeting the hurdle has a significant downside impact. Likewise, achieving the hurdle has a significant positive upside impact.

Vocabulary Alert. While the two terms *threshold* and *hurdle* sound alike, they are not the same. A threshold is a minimum level of performance for one measure that must be achieved before payments are earned on that measure. A hurdle ties the payout of one measure to performance accomplishment on a second measure. Here is an application of these words: "You must meet the *threshold* of the quota before any payout can be earned." "Your commission earnings on all sales will be increased 10 percent if you meet or exceed the weighted average 35 percent gross margin *hurdle*."

Sales Representative, Example 5B: Link Variable Commission—Hurdle

Figure 5-27 is an example of a variable commission rate featuring a hurdle. While the payout schedule is not capped, the upside commission rates are not available unless the hurdle is met.

Component	Link Variable Commission—Hurdle

Commission Rate	Hurdle: All products must be at 75% of quota, before the second commission rate can be earned on any product.
	
	Product Categories
	             Digital Component Service
	             Products Assemblies Contracts
	1st Commission Rate 4% 2% 10%
	2nd Commission Rate 6% 3% 15%

Figure 5-27. Variable Commission Rate with Hurdle

Observations

Hurdles are easy to understand. One limitation is that they are like an on/off switch. Either the sales representative reaches the hurdle or he or she does not.

Sales Representative TI-Commission: 5B. Link Commission—Multiplier

Like other linked techniques, a multiplier requires two or more measures (see Figure 5-28). A multiplier provides greater pay discrimination than a hurdle. The payout impact of the multiplier varies

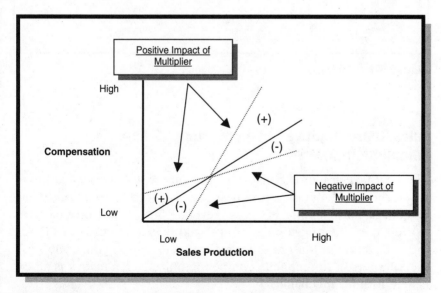

Figure 5-28. Sales Rep: 5B. Link Commission—Multiplier

given the performance range of the individual. A multiplier provides very clear direction on the importance of the first and second measure.

Observations

As Figure 5-29 illustrates, the payout impact is both positive (did exceed goal on the second measure) and negative (did not exceed goal on the second measure). Some organizations prefer to have only a positive multiplier with no take-away of a negative deduction.

Component	Link Commission—Multiplier		
Measure 1: Commission Rate	1st Commission Rate 2nd Commission Rate	**Performance To Goal** To 100% Above 100%	**Commission Rate** 7% 12%
Measure 2: Commission Multiplier	**Performance to Goal on 2^{nd}Measure** Above 120% 110% to 119% 105% to 109% 100% to 104% 95% to 99% 90% to 94% 80% to 89% Below 80%	**Multiplier of Measure 1 Commission Earnings** 130% 120% 110% 100% 95% 80% 75% 50%	

Figure 5-29. Link Commission—Multiplier

Sales Representative TI-Commission: 5C. Link Commission—Matrix

The final link design is a matrix (see Figure 5-30). Matrices are used when the company asks the salesperson to resolve two competing objectives. For example: (1) grow revenue but (2) sell profitably; or (1) retain existing customers but (2) add new customers; or (1) sell the core business but (2) sell new products, too. Anytime you wish the salesperson to reconcile competing objectives, a matrix is an excellent formula mechanic.

Percentage of Sales Revenue Dollars/Month

Excellence	2.0	3.0	3.9	4.9	5.9	6.7	7.4	8.2	9.0
	1.8	2.8	3.7	4.7	5.7	6.3	7.0	7.7	8.3
	1.6	2.5	3.5	4.5	5.4	6.0	6.6	7.1	7.7
	1.3	2.3	3.3	4.3	5.2	5.7	6.1	6.6	7-0
Target	1.1	2.1	2.1	4.0	5.0	6.3	5.7	6.0	6.3
	0.8	1.7	2.5	3.3	4.2	4.5	4.8	5.2	5.5
	0.6	1.3	1.9	2,6	3.3	3.7	4.0	4.3	4.7
	0.3	0.8	1.4	1.9	2.5	2.8	3.2	3.5	3.8
Threshold	0.0	.04	.08	1.3	1.7	2.0	2.3	2.7	3.0

Sales Volume to Goal (row axis label)

Threshold   Target   Excellence

Average Gross Margin to Goal

Figure 5-30. Sales Rep: 5C. Link Commission—Matrix

With a matrix, the salesperson—who in this case has pricing latitude—needs to sell over target and with a high average gross margin
to be eligible for commission rates greater than 5 percent. Exceptional
performance on both measures (volume and average gross margin)
can provide a commission rate as high as 9 percent for all sales revenue.

Note the following features of a matrix:

- The salesperson must resolve two conflicting measures—in this
  case, sales volume versus profits.

- There is a double threshold at the low end.

- Average gross margin has a higher importance weighting in the matrix than sales volume goal attainment. Average gross margin is
  weighted 60 percent, and sales volume goal attainment is weighted
  40 percent in the matrix.

- Target "quota" can be the same for all salespeople, assuming territories are of equal size and opportunity, or can vary by salesperson.

- Matrices are normally constructed with an odd number of rows and
  columns to provide a middle cell for presenting target performance
  and incentive rate. Most matrices are at least 9×9 and some are as
  large as 15×15.

Observations

Matrices are ideally suited to provide rewards when there are two competing measures. Because of matrices' visual displays, salespeople readily understand how their performance impacts their pay.

Hurting profits by rewarding profits. Senior management was perplexed to learn that the gross profit measure in the incentive plan actually hurt profits. *Distribution companies sell what others manufacture. Multiline wholesalers purchase products from numerous manufacturers, bring them into inventory, and sell to the local market. The key measure of sales success is gross margin dollars—sales price less loaded cost of goods. Management correctly provided sales personnel with pricing flexibility to meet competitive pressures. To reward high sales with high pricing, management structured the incentive plan to pay a flat commission rate on all gross margin dollars. Unfortunately, it had the unintended consequence of reducing pricing. Why? Rather than keep prices high and risk losing the sale, sales personnel would reduce pricing to save the order. A commission on a few gross margin dollars is better than a commission on no gross margin dollars. Preferred Solution: Create a payout schedule that pays a higher commission rate on gross margin dollars for orders with higher gross margin percent.*

Providing Equal Earning Opportunities When Territories Are Dissimilar in Size

Individual Commission Rate

As noted earlier, commission formula pays an established rate for sales production (for example, revenue, gross margins, or units sold). The commission schedule is constant for all sales personnel in the same position. (Individual quotas may affect access to different ramp levels, but, for the most part, payments are similar for similar levels of sales production.) Target incentive commission plans require territories to have similar sales potential. Sales organizations use account assignment and reassignment to keep territories balanced.

Organizations with the latitude to make account changes can easily keep earnings comparable by equalizing the sales-loading among sales personnel through account reassignments. This is not a preferred practice for income producers, but in the case of sales representatives, managing territory size through account assignments ensures that target incentive pay opportunities remain comparable among sales personnel. However, in many instances, it's not plausible to reassign accounts. In these cases, the movement of accounts is disruptive to customers and sales personnel. Simple geographic realities do not always allow for reassignment to other sales personnel.

As territory size becomes more dissimilar, the use of commission programs becomes more problematic. The eventual solution is the use of a bonus formula method that pays a percent of target incentive as a percent of quota accomplishment. Prior to adopting a bonus formula, two methods can extend the utility of commission rates: individual commission rates and sales force stratification.

Sales Representative TI-Commission: 6A. Individual Commission Rates

An individual commission rate (ICR) provides each person with his or her own commission rate. The purpose of ICRs is to manage payouts to a similar target incentive amount even though territories are dissimilar in size.

Sales management creates an ICR for each salesperson by dividing that person's target incentive amount (which may be unique for him or her) by the unique quota sales volume expected for the territory.

Figure 5-31 illustrates how to calculate ICR.

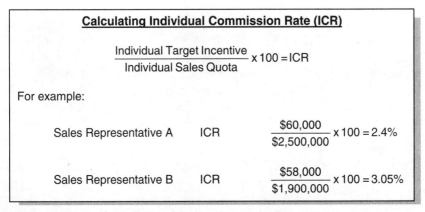

Figure 5-31. Individual Commission Rate Calculation

In this manner, sales management assigns an individual ICR to each salesperson.
Figure 5-32 is the incentive plan for ICR.

Component	ICR Commission Schedule		
Commission Rates	1st Commission Rate 2nd Commission Rate	**Quota Performance** 0 – 100% Over 100%	**Commission Rate** ICR% ICR% x 1.5

Figure 5-32. ICR Commission Schedule

An interesting variation on this design is to provide an ICR for each salesperson up to quota. But once past quota, all sales personnel in the same job get the same commission rate. This hybrid model (see Figure 5-33) helps to equalize dissimilar-sized territories up to quota performance. But once above quota, dissimilar-sized territories now pay out according to actual performance, and pay opportunity is not equalized by using an ICR.

Component	ICR and Commission Rate—Hybrid		
Commission Rates	1st Commission Rate 2nd Commission Rate	**Quota Performance** 0 – 100% Over 100%	**Commission Rate** ICR% 7%

Figure 5-33. ICR and Commission Rate—Hybrid Model

ICR-Commission or Bonus? An ICR has all the outward appearances of a commission payment for each occurrence. However, it accomplishes what a bonus formula does—equalizing the earning opportunity regardless of the size of the territory.

Observations

ICR provides a transition formula technique between commission and bonus formulas. Most companies eventually adopt a commission plan after several years with an ICR program.

Sales Representative TI-Commission: 6B.
Stratified Commission Rates

This final commission technique for sales representatives is not really a unique commission formula, but, instead, a method to use commission plans for a stratified sales organization.

Sales force stratification segments customers into categories such as size and/or potential. For example, the larger opportunities are placed in global accounts, mid-sized accounts are grouped into major accounts, and the remaining smaller accounts are grouped by geographic territories and may be labeled as general business.

Stratification groups sales territories by size. From a sales compensation perspective, this configuration supports the use of commission plans because territories of like size are grouped in the same category. Each job category has its own commission rate correctly sized to the volume opportunity and target incentive opportunity for that category. Figure 5-34 shows that the larger territories have lower commission rates than the smaller territories. However, the volumes are much larger, assuring a higher payout for the large territories, even though the effective commission rate is lower.

Component	Commission Rates by Stratified Sales Segment		
		Below Quota	Equal & Above Quota
Commission Rates	Global Account Executives	1.5%	2.0%
	Major Account Managers	3.0%	4.5%
	Territory Sales Representatives	6.0%	8.5%

Figure 5-34. Commission Rates by Stratified Sales Segments

Observations

Stratification can provide the right type of payouts, but defending the lower rates for higher positions will require continual explanation.

Bonus Formula

As we have seen, commission pay plans provide an absolute rate for sales production. Bonus formula techniques, on the other hand, pay for relative performance against a percent of quota attainment. In this manner, actual sales production is translated to a percent of quota accomplishment and the payout rate is expressed as a function of this performance to goal percent.

Figure 5-35 illustrates how bonus formula equalizes earning opportunities.

Territories	Sales Volume	Incentive Payment at 100% to Quota
Territory A	$4,500,000	$40,000
Territory B	$2,300,000	$40,000
Territory C	$9,300,000	$40,000

Figure 5-35. Bonus Formula Technique Example

A bonus formula allows sales management to pay for sales results as a percent of quota rather than a percent of actual sales production. There are numerous reasons for doing this, but the most compelling reason is that actual sales volume production does not always equate to sales efforts. For example, the size of large territories may be a function of account buying patterns rather than the persuasive selling skills of the salesperson.

To equalize earning opportunities and to be considered a bonus formula, the following must be present:

- A target incentive earning amount, such as a flat dollar amount, percent of base salary, percent of total target compensation, or percent of a pool of monies

- A quota

- An incentive formula expressed as a portion of the target incentive amount for percent accomplishment of target quota

In all the examples that follow, sales production is expressed as a percent of 100 percent to quota and not actual dollar, margin, or unit sales as illustrated in Figure 5-36.

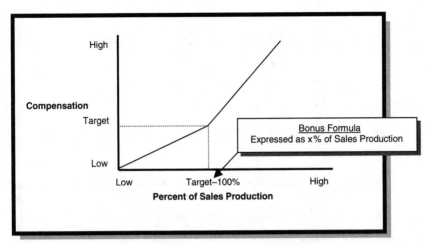

Figure 5-36. Bonus Formula: Expressed as Performance to 100% of Goal

Sales Representative TI-Bonus sample plan designs that will be described include:

7. Bonus Formula—Step

8. Bonus Formula—Rate

9A. Link Bonus—Hurdle

9B. Link Bonus—Multiplier

9C. Link Bonus—Matrix

10. Bonus with Drop-In Commission

11. Management by Objective (MBO)/Key Sales Objective (KSO) Plan

Sales Representative: 7. Bonus Formula–Step

The most common bonus application is the step bonus formula (see Figure 5-37). Higher earnings, expressed as a percent of the target incentive, are provided for higher percent performance to quota on a step basis.

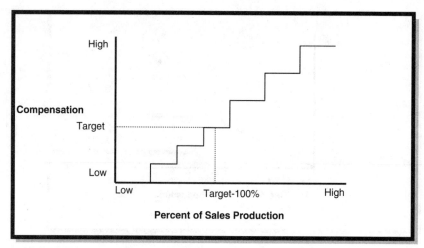

Figure 5-37. Sales Rep: 7. Step-Based Bonus

This step bonus formula (see Figure 5-38) has a threshold and a cap. There is no interpretation between steps. Performance between steps pays the rate of the lower step.

Component	Bonus Formula—Step	
Part 1: Base Salary	**Annual Base Salary** $65,000	
Part 2: Bonus Schedule	Bonus paid as a percent of base salary: **Sales Performance** **Percent to Goal** 150% and over 125% to 149% 110% to 124% 105% to 109% 100% to 104% 90% to 99% 80% to 89% Below 80%	**Bonus: % of** **Base Salary** 105% 85% 65% 50% 35% 15% 5% 0

Figure 5-38. Step Bonus Formula

Figure 5-39 is the same structure but uses target incentive instead of base salary as the payout basis.

Component	Bonus Formula—Step	
Part 1: Base Salary	**Annual Target Incentive** $22,750	
Part 2: Bonus Schedule	Bonus paid as a percent of target incentive: **Sales Performance Percent to Goal** 150% and over 125% to 149% 110% to 124% 105% to 109% 100% to 104% 90% to 99% 80% to 89% Below 80%	**Bonus: % of Target Incentive** 300% 245% 185% 142% 100% 45% 15% 0

Figure 5-39. Step Bonus Formula Using Target Incentive

In both step bonus formulas presented, the payout amounts are very similar. The only change is the basis used for the target incentive—base salary is used in the first example and target incentive is used in the second example. Both approaches are effective. One elevates the importance of the base salary, while the other ignores the base salary and places significant emphasis on the target incentive amount. When using the target incentive amount, the dollars can be equal for all sales personnel in the same job or can vary based on sales management's value of the territory and contribution of the salesperson.

Observations

A step bonus formula is a popular means to equalize territories and provide varying payouts based on quota performance. The use of steps usually occurs when the performance range is wide and quota-setting confidence is moderate.

Sales Representative: 8. Bonus Formula—Rate

Use a bonus formula rate (see Figures 5-40 to 5-42) to eliminate the cap and gaps in payout steps, which are both prominent features of the step bonus formula.

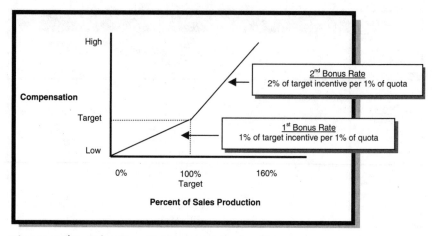

Figure 5-40. Sales Rep: 8. Bonus Formula—Rate

Component	Bonus Formula—Rate	
Part 1: Target Incentive	**Annual Target Incentive** $25,000	
Part 2: Bonus Rate	Bonus paid as a percent of target incentive: 	**Bonus Payout Rate**
	Below Quota	Each 1 percent of quota, 1% of target incentive
	At or Above Quota	Each 1 percent of quota, 2% of target incentive

Figure 5-41. Bonus Formula Rate

Figure 5-42 illustrates the payout for the formula presented in Figure 5-41 for three levels of performance: 50%, 100%, and 125%.

	Sales Result	Payout	Calculation
	50%	$12,500	50% x $25,000 = $12,500
or			
	100%	$25,000	100% x $25,000 = $25,000
or			
	125%	$37,500	(100% x $25,000) + (2% x 25 x $25,000) = $37,500

Figure 5-42. Sample Bonus Payouts for Bonus Formula—Rate

The bonus formula rate allows for payment over the full range of quota performance.

Observations

A bonus formula rate has the positive benefits of an uncapped plan similar to a commission program. However, it does require a two-step calculation to arrive at the incentive earning.

Bonus Linked Designs

Bonus plans can use the same linkage methods as commission plans, such as hurdles, multipliers, and matrices.

Sales Representative: 9A. Link Bonus—Hurdle

Bonus plans can use hurdles to tie two or more performance measures together. As illustrated in Figure 5-43, the retention rate of current customers acts as a hurdle affecting the bonus payout schedule.

Component	Link Bonus—Hurdle		
Part 1: Base Salary	**Salary Range/Year**		
	Minimum $56,000	**Midpoint** $70,000	**Maximum** $84,000
Part 2: Bonus Schedule	Bonus paid as a percent of midpoint: **Sales Performance** **Percent to Goal** **Bonus: % of** **Base Salary** 115% and over 75% 110% to 114% 55% 105% to 109% 40% 100% to 104% 25% 90% to 99% 20% 80% to 89% 15% Below 80% 0 Hurdle: No incentive can be earned past 100% of goal unless the retention rate is greater than 80% of last year's sales revenue from existing customers.		

Figure 5-43. Link Bonus with Hurdle

Observations

The hurdle in Figure 5-43 imposes a significant punitive treatment for not surpassing 80 percent of revenue retention. No additional pay can be earned past 100 percent of goal.

Sales Representative: 9B. Link Bonus–Multiplier

In Figure 5-44, a bonus rate formula gains a product mix multiplier to help reward cross-selling of products.

Component	Link Bonus Formula Rate—Multiplier
Part 1: Target Incentive	**Annual Target Incentive** $25,000
Part 2: Bonus Rate	Bonus paid as a percent of target incentive: **Bonus Payout Rate** Below Quota Each 1 percent of quota, 1% of target incentive At or Above Quota Each 1 percent of quota, 2% of target incentive
Part 3: Multiplier	Product mix multiplier is applied to the Bonus Rate payout: **Number of** **Product Mix** **Products** **Multiplier Times** **Reaching Goal** **Bonus Payout** 5 of 5 120% 4 of 5 110% 3 of 5 100% 2 of 5 90% 1 of 5 75%

Figure 5-44. Link Bonus Formula Rate with Multiplier

Observations

Using a product mix multiplier with both upside opportunity and downside risk notifies the salesperson that cross-selling or achieving product mix goals is very important.

Sales Representative: 9C. Link Bonus–Matrix

A bonus matrix, like a commission matrix, features two competing objectives. In Figure 5-45, the two measures are sales volume and price realization. Price realization is a measure of how close to list price the salesperson sells the product. The use of this measure is appropriate when the salesperson has some degree of pricing authority.

Percent of Quarterly Target Incentive

80.0	98.3	116.7	135.0	153.3	190.0	226.7	263.3	**300.0**
66.7	85.0	103.3	121.7	140.0	169.6	199.2	228.8	258.3
53.3	71.7	90.0	108.3	126.7	149.2	171.7	194.2	216.7
40.0	58.3	76.7	95.0	113.3	128.8	144.2	159.6	175.0
26.7	**45.0**	63.3	**81.7**	**100.0**	108.3	116.7	125.0	133.3
20.0	34.8	49.6	64.4	**79.2**	87.5	95.8	104.2	112.5
13.3	24.6	35.8	47.1	**58.3**	66.7	75.0	83.3	91.7
6.7	14.4	22.1	29.8	**37.5**	45.8	54.2	62.5	70.8
0.0	4.2	8.3	12.5	**16.7**	25.0	33.3	41.7	**50.0**

Excellence

Sales Volume   Target
% to Target   100%

Threshold

Threshold   Target–100%   Excellence

**Price Realization
% to Target**

Figure 5-45. 9C. Matrix Bonus Formula

Observations

In the bonus matrix illustrated in Figure 5-45, we see that sales volume has a higher incentive weighting than price realization. This design has a double threshold and a double cap at the top end. The salesperson cannot earn greater than 300 percent of his or her target incentive.

Sales Representative: 10. Bonus with Drop-In Commission

Sometimes sales management will need the use of a hybrid bonus and commission plan (see Figure 5-46). An example is the drop-in commission rate. This technique uses a bonus formula to reward quota performance, but provides a drop-in commission rate to recognize and reward larger sales territories.

Observations

The reason this technique is called a *drop-in* is that it provides additional sales rewards for a defined range—in this case, starting at $2,000,000 and terminating at $5,000,000.

Component	Bonus/Commission Hybrid	
Part 1: Base Salary	Base Salary/Year $65,000	
Part 2: Bonus Schedule	Bonus paid as a percent of base salary: **Sales Performance Percent to Goal** **Bonus: % of Base Salary**	

Sales Performance Percent to Goal	Bonus: % of Base Salary
150% and over	105%
125% to 149%	85%
110% to 124%	65%
105% to 109%	50%
100% to 104%	35%
90% to 99%	15%
80% to 89%	5%
Below 80%	0

Part 3: Drop-in Commission Rate	Drop-in Commission Rate (per Net Sales Revenue)
	Sales Volume Between $2,000,000 and $5,000,000
Drop-in Commission Rate	1.5%

Figure 5-46. Hybrid Bonus and Commission Plan

Sales Representative: 11. Management by Objective/Key Sales Objective

In some instances, sales management needs to create unique incentive objectives for individual sales personnel. The use of a Management by Objectives (MBO) component provides the flexibility to craft unique measures per salesperson. Although MBOs have a long history in the corporate environment, the sales force has recently adapted the MBO concept for sales situations. Key Sales Objectives (KSOs) provide a handy framework for sales executives to develop incentive payouts tied to individual performance.

Here are some of the design considerations when creating a KSO program:

- Balance KSOs by not letting any single measure be worth more than 50 percent and not less than 10 percent
- Limit KSO measures to five or fewer
- Select measures that impact sales results and are quantitative
- Provide KSO visibility through a database accessible by senior sales management

- Require two levels of supervisor review before final KSO objectives are established and payouts are made

- Require two levels of supervisor review for any modifications during the program period

A preferred method is to use a point system to assign and calculate the KSO values and payout scores (see Figure 5-47). One method is to create a 200-point maximum scoring scheme with 100 being considered par, or expected performance. The KSO worksheet can divide up the value of the points depending on the weighting of the KSO performance measures.

Elements	#1	#2	#3	#4	#5	Total
	KSO Commitments and Scoring Sheet					
Factor	New Customers	Pre-Packaged Solutions	Target Discount Rate	Cancelled Orders	Customer HQ Visits	
Commitment Objectives	7 over $500K in Sales	15 Signed Contracts	8%	<5%	5/Qrtr	
Weighting	20%	25%	25%	15%	15%	
Point Value (A)	20 pts	25 pts	25 pts	15 pts	15 pts	
Performance to Goal (B)	110%	120%	85%	75%	50%	
Performance Point Value A x B =	22	30	21.25	11.25	7.5	92
Performance Comments						
Authorization	Date:					

Figure 5-47. KSO Commitments and Scoring Sheet

Figure 5-48 illustrates the conversion of points to dollars.

Observations

The target incentive amount can vary by salesperson. The KSO program is capped, which is a normal feature of KSO plans. Most KSOs are set quarterly, semiannually, or annually.

Component	KSO Point Payout Schedule	
Target Incentive	**KSO Target Incentive** $5,000	

Component	Points	Percent of Target Incentive
KSO Payout Schedule	175 – 200	150%
	150 – 174	125%
	125 – 149	110%
	105 – 125	105%
	95 – 104	100%
	75 – 94	75%
	50 – 74	25%
	below 50	0

Figure 5-48. KSO Point Payout Schedule

Formulas for Sales Teams

Many sales organizations need to provide sales support to customers using a team approach. Sales team members contribute to the successful sale of products, services, and solutions to the customer. There are two types of sales teams: *Dedicated Sales Teams* and *Opportunity Sales Teams*.

Below are three examples of team formulas:

12A. Dedicated Sales Team—Specialist Model

12B. Dedicated Sales Team—Collaborative Model

12C. Opportunity Sales Team—Event Awards

13. Base Salary Step Plan

Dedicated Sales Teams

Dedicated sales teams have members that are permanently assigned to a work team. A dedicated sales team is typically led by a senior sales representative such as an account executive. Depending on the sales coverage model, the team may include the following personnel: additional sales representatives, technical presales support, contract management, fulfillment administration, installation personnel, and customer service. Several incentive formula types support dedicated sales team efforts.

Sales Representative: 12A. Dedicated Sales Team—Specialist Model

A dedicated sales team has full-time members. A dedicated sales team can exhibit varying degrees of "team-ing-ness." The specialist model is the least team-centric sales model. The leader of the sales unit, the account executive, orchestrates team efforts through the assignment of duties to team specialists. Each specialist contributes to the final sales results by performing his or her assigned duties. This type of team features a classic command-and-control model consistent with typical types of hierarchical work units. The incentive plan for the team members is illustrated in Figure 5-49.

Jobs	Incentive Elements	Weighting
Account Executive	Total Account Sales Volume*	60%
	Account Profitability	25%
	Individual KSOs	15%
Sales Representatives	Total Account Sales Volume*	45%
	Assigned Unit Sales Volume	40%
	Individual KSOs	15%
Presales Support	Total Account Sales Volume*	75%
	Individual KSOs	25%
Customer Service	Total Account Sales Volume*	75%
	Individual KSOs	25%
*Shared goal among all team specialists		

Figure 5-49. Sales Team: 12A. Individual Specialists

In Figure 5-49, each team member shares at least one team measure: total account sales. While each person has his or her own incentive plan, by sharing a common goal, the program provides support to a team goal.

Sales Representative: 12B. Dedicated Sales Team—Collaborative Model

The collaborative team model as illustrated in Figure 5-50 uses joint decision-making and work content sharing to achieve a shared goal. These collaborative sales teams see team members as co-equals. The

Component	Team ScheduleCollaborative		
Part 1: Base Salary Range		**Base Salary Range**	
		Minimum	Midpoint	Maximum

		Minimum	Midpoint	Maximum
Account Executive $	$xx,xxx	$xx,xxx	$xx,xxx
Sales Representatives	$xx,xxx	$xx,xxx	$xx,xxx
Presales Support	$xx,xxx	$xx,xxx	$xx,xxx
Customer Service	$xx,xxx	$xx,xxx	$xx,xxx

Part 2: Annual Sales Team Award

Annual Sales Team Award
Percent of Base Salary Midpoint

Sales Volume Target:

3.0	3.9	4.8	5.6	6.5	7.4	8.3	9.1	10.0
2.6	3.5	4.4	5.3	6.1	6.9	7.6	8.4	9.1
2.3	3.1	4.0	4.9	5.8	6.4	7.0	7.6	8.3
1.9	2.8	3.6	4.5	5.4	5.9	6.4	6.9	7.4
1.5	2.4	3.3	4.1	5.0	5.4	5.8	6.1	6.5
0	0	0	0	4.1	4.5	4.9	5.3	5.6
0	0	0	0	3.3	3.6	4.0	4.4	4.8
0	0	0	0	2.4	2,8	3.1	3.5	3.9
0	0	0	0	1.5	1.9	2.3	2.6	3.0

Target

Figure 5-50. 12B. Collaborative Team Model

appropriate sales compensation program supports this management model by providing the same reward structure that applies to all team members.

Observations

All team members share in the same team award. This shared matrix approach supports a preferred collaborative management approach. If desired, to achieve absolute egalitarianism, configure the matrix with actual dollars so that payouts are equal regardless of job assignment.

Opportunity Sales Team

Many sales teams are assembled to meet emerging customer-buying opportunities. These teams are not permanent, but temporarily configured to prepare a customer proposal and to present the company's complete value proposition. Normally, the specialists assigned to these teams participate in a gainsharing plan or other corporate team program, or simply are paid a base salary with annual merit adjustments. Select companies, however, like to provide an award to these individuals for assisting with a sales effort. Often, these pay plans are add-on spot awards.

Sales Representative: 12C. Opportunity Sales Team—Event Awards

A common payout method for opportunity teams is an event award paid at the time of a significant event such as a contract signing as shown in Figure 5-51.

Paid at Contract Acceptance

	Contract Value		
	$2M – $5M	$5M – 15M	>$15M
Presales Support Specialist	$100	$150	$250
Contracts Specialist	$75	$125	$175
Service Coordinator	$75	$125	$175
Installation Specialist	$50	$75	$100

Figure 5-51. Sales Team: 12C. Team Incentive Awards

Observations

These nominal rewards provide recognition for sales support during the sales process. The account executive and sales personnel would be on a normal sales compensation program.

Using Base Salary Only

In most cases, sales compensation—the use of variable pay tied to sales results—is the primary means to reward sales personnel. However, some sales departments do not wish to use variable compensation to recognize sales results. The base salary program provides some latitude for recognizing sales results.

The merit pay system provides one means to recognize sales results. The annual increase program can be calibrated to reward those with higher sales results. Another method is to provide pay steps for sustained sales performance.

Sales Representative: 13. Base Salary Step Plan

In a base salary step plan, higher levels of base salary are available for those who sustain a predetermined sales level. In the simplest model, as illustrated in Figure 5-52, the base salary for the new year is established by sales performance in the previous year.

Component	Base Salary Step Pay Plan	
	Last Year Sales Performance	**This Year Base Salary Amount**
Salary Steps	Below $1M	$65,000
	$1M–$3M	$70,000
	$3M–$5M	$95,000
	Over $5M	$110,000

Figure 5-52. 13. Base Salary Step Plan

Observations

Varying the base salary depending on the previous year's performance provides a good reward to excel. Unfortunately, for these models to work effectively, base pay must be reduced if the level of sales performance drops into a lower category. This event will most likely trigger significant terminations. For some professional service firms, sales results are rewarded with promotions and eventual partnership without the use of sales compensation.

Summary

While the list of incentive formulas in this chapter seems extensive and complete, it actually only represents the building blocks of incentive formula design. The combination of these different components gives the full palette of choices. The number of configurations is almost unlimited. However, limiting the number of performance measures to three or fewer precludes the occurrence of overly complex designs.

6

Formula Construction

Sales compensation formula construction is all about mathematics. Fortunately, it's not very complex and is easily mastered. First, we will examine the fundamentals of constructing sales compensation formulas. Then, we will examine the economics of sales compensation for income producers. Finally, we will examine how to build target incentive commission and bonus formulas for sales representatives.

Fundamentals of Sales Compensation Formulas

$$\frac{\text{compensation}}{\text{performance}} = \text{payout rate}$$

The payout rate is calculated by dividing the compensation amount by the performance amount.

Using our payout graph (see Figure 6-1), we see the target compensation is $100,000 and the expected performance is $2,000,000.

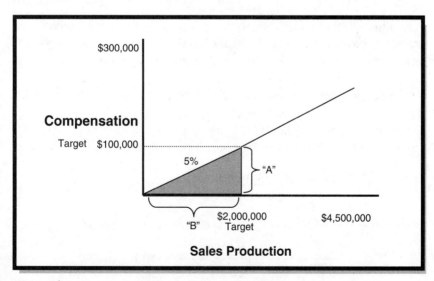

Figure 6-1. Flat Commission—Formula Graph

The formula to calculate the payout rate (also known as the *slope* in the math world) is to simply divide the pay by the performance, or A divided by B, presented as a calculation:

$$\frac{A\ compensation}{B\ performance} = payout\ rate\ (slope)$$

Here is the formula expressed as numbers:

$$\frac{\$100,000}{\$2,000,000} \times 100 = 5\%$$

Multiply by 100 to move the decimal point to change the resulting division outcome from .05 to 5% for notation purposes.

The flat commission schedule (see Figure 6-2) displays the sales compensation plan when published for sales personnel.

Component	Flat Commission Schedule	
	Sales Performance	**Commission Rate**
Commission Rate	All Sales	5%

Figure 6-2. Flat Commission Schedule

As illustrated in Figure 6-3, to calculate a second (progressive or regressive) payout rate, simply replicate the same calculation for the new upside pay opportunity and expected upside performance range.

The second payout rate is calculated using the same formula model. Because the first payout rate of 5% paid $100,000 for the first performance range of $2,000,000, eliminate these numbers from the equation when calculating the second payout rate.

$$\frac{C\ compensation}{D\ performance} = payout\ rate$$

Or, the actual numbers:

$$\frac{\$300,000 - \$100,000}{\$4,500,000 - \$2,000,000} \times 100 = 8\%$$

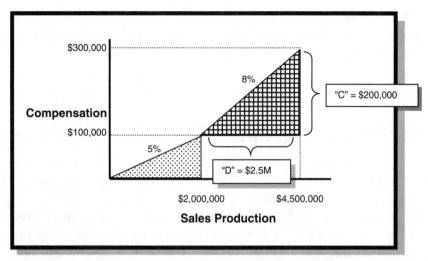

Figure 6-3. Straight Commission 2nd Rate—Formula Graph

The subtractions of $100,000 of target pay and $2,000,000 for target performance leaves the following division of upside compensation divided by upside performance:

$$\frac{\$200,000}{\$2,500,000} \times 100 = 8\%$$

The incentive plan pays 5 cents for every dollar of sales up to and including $2,000,000 and 8 cents for every dollar over $2,000,000 in sales. Figure 6-4 displays this commission schedule.

Component	Progressive Ramp Commission Schedule		
		Sales Performance	Commission Rate
Commission Rate	1st Commission Rate	To $2M	5%
	2nd Commission Rate	Over $2M	8%

Figure 6-4. Progressive Ramp Commission Schedule

For sales efforts that achieve $2,000,000 in sales, the payout is $100,000. For those sellers who close $4,500,000 in business, the sales compensation program will pay $300,000.

We will use this same fundamental formula calculation method when we construct compensation formulas for income producers and sales representatives including both TI-Commission and TI-Bonus formulas.

The Economics of Income Producers

The sales compensation plans for income producers should be simple: a fixed commission rate (flat) for all sales revenue. In some industries, the commission rate for income producers is so well established that few in sales management would even presume to question the rate, let alone alter it. Senior management simply accepts the rate for the income producers as a known constant built right into business planning assumptions of the company's financial model. However, like any economic statement, market forces have an ongoing influence on the development and refinement of income producer commission rates. No one should assume that commission rates are constant and cannot be changed.

As we examined earlier, income producers are independent sellers who have access to customers. Their economic value is their ability to reach and influence buyers. Companies pay for this access by paying a commission for sales results. Most income producers' pay plans feature a flat (unchanging) commission rate. It's not unusual for the income producer to be a nonpayroll employee paid as a contract worker or separate business entity. Regardless of the legal relationship, there is a rational basis for setting and evaluating the commission rates paid to income producers.

Income producer commission rates vary by industry. While this is not an exact science, the trend is clear. Industries with high volumes per income producer tend to have lower commission rates, and industries with lower volumes per producer tend to have higher commission rates. Management should constantly examine the expected volumes to determine if the commission rates are still effective, too high, or too low. In Figure 6-5 we see that commission rates differ by industry depending on the expected volume per income producer.

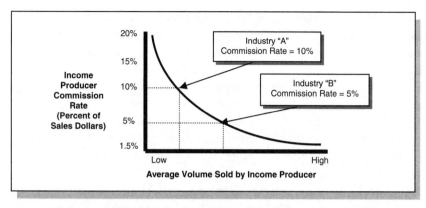

Figure 6-5. Commission Rates for Income Producers Vary by Sales Volume

For one type of income producer—the independent manufacturer representatives—the loss of the product line is a major, ongoing concern. A company has the option of replacing the independent reps with an in-house dedicated sales force. When this occurs, this is known as "taking the line direct." At a certain point, it may make more economic sense to terminate the independent reps and hire a company sales force. As shown in Figure 6-6, a financial analysis of the "switching point" will identify when it's better to use one sales coverage model versus another.

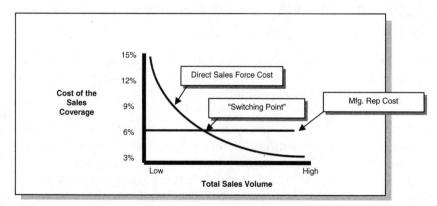

Figure 6-6. Cost of Sales for Income Producers versus Direct Sales Force

As the overall volume of the line increases, it becomes more economically feasible to hire a direct sales force, particularly for large, ongoing purchases. This, of course, assumes that the direct sales force can establish buyer relationships and successfully displace the independent (income producer) reps. To calculate the switching point correctly, include both direct and indirect costs. Don't forget to add loss of sales during the changeover as a cost factor, too.

For some industries, historic commission rates seem to remain constant. In parts of the United States, the commission rate for residential real estate is 6 percent of the house sale price. The actual commission rate paid to the agent who sells your house is 1.5 percent. Three percent is assigned to the listing broker and 3 percent is assigned to the selling broker. The listing broker and the agent split the 3 percent, so the agent's actual commission rate is 1.5 percent of the sales price.

Certain electronic component segments pay a flat 10 percent to the manufacturer reps for all sales. Mass reach apparel can pay as low as 2 percent, whereas specialty apparel can pay as high as 15 percent. However, practices do vary from these norms and what the market will bear allows for a give and take in actual commission rates.

Most industries that maintain a constant income producer commission rate exhibit one of two traits: Either the market segment is very stable (food brokers) or employment levels vary greatly with market swings such as in real estate and stock brokerage.

Advanced Thinking about Income Producer Commission Rates

We suggest that companies consider the following adjustments to the traditional flat commission formula for income producers when presented with the following conditions:

- *Increase commission rates if the income producer is instrumental in adding substantial incremental growth.* Reward the economic contribution of the income producers when they singularly drive new revenue growth. Provide a progressive commission rate for these new dollars. A progressive ramp commission schedule motivates additional sales, recognizes contribution, and helps contribute to seller loyalty. Figure 6-7 is an illustration of a progressive

Component	Progressive Ramp Participation Rate			
	Commission Rate to Agency Varies by Product, Between 5% and 10%.			
Participation Rate		**Seller Performance**	**Commission Split**	
			Seller	**Agency**
	1st Participation Rate	To $5M	20%	80%
	2nd Participation Rate	$5M–$7.5M	22%	78%
	3rd Participation Rate	Over $7.5M	25%	75%

Figure 6-7. Progressive Ramp Participation Rate

participation rate for an income producer. The agency (employer) gets a commission for selling a product line, in this case, 5 to 10 percent of the sale price. The principal of the agency then in turn splits this with the sellers who work for the agency. This split is known as the participation rate.

Figure 6-8 is the method used to calculate the participation rate.

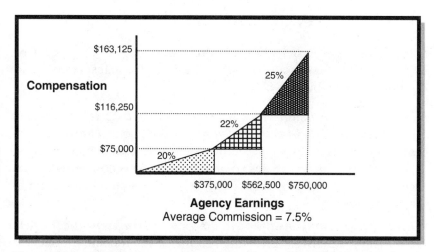

Figure 6-8. Progressive Ramp Rate—Calculation Participation Rate

Figure 6-9 presents the formula for calculating the participation (share of the agency's commissions).

| Participation Rate Schedule | | | |
Agency Commissions	Avg. Agency Commission 7.5% of Actual Revenue	Target Payment to Income Producer	Percent Participation Rate
$5,000,000	$375,000	$75,000	20%
$7,500,000	$562,500	$116,250	22%
$10,000,000	$750,000	$163,125	25%

Figure 6-9. Participation Rate Schedule

The first participation rate is calculated as follows:

$$\frac{\$75,000}{\$375,000} \times 100 = 20\%$$

The second participation rate is calculated as follows:

$$\frac{\$116,250 - \$75,000}{\$562,500 - \$375,000} \times 100 = 22\%$$

The third participation rate is calculated as follows:

$$\frac{\$163,125 - \$116,250}{\$750,000 - \$562,000} \times 100 = 25\%$$

Increasing the participation rate from 20 to 22 to 25 percent recognizance, in this case, is the pivotal role of the salesperson in securing additional business.

- *Decrease commission rates as volume increases when income producer is incidental to added growth.* While a regressive commission rate schedule may be motivationally challenging, in situations where additional sales volume (bluebirds) is not caused by exceptional sales efforts, then using regressive commission rates is appropriate.

- *Reduce sales compensation credits for recurring revenue.* Review crediting practices for recurring revenue. If the income producer is instrumental in maintaining and reselling the recurring revenue, then include all recurring revenue in incentive calculations. If recurring revenue is inherent in the original sale and does not require hands-on attention by the salesperson, reduce or discount recurring revenue. Consider terminating, after a period of time, the revenue credit on recurring revenue if the income producer's influence is inconsequential.

- *Establish a tiered producer program.* A tiered program provides different categories of commission participation depending on levels of performance, investment, certification, and exclusivity, for example, Platinum, Gold, and Silver, or I, II, and III. Tiered programs allow differentiated commission treatment.

Unlimited earnings—means just that: unlimited. The president of a privately held investment company was dismayed to learn that the top salesperson was to earn incentive payments five times what was expected. What was he to do? *After years of lackluster performance, a new management team was brought in to revitalize the commercial real estate unit. With an uncapped incentive plan, the new team produced sales results in excess of any conceivable level. Now, faced with making payments far in excess of intended levels, what should the president do? Preferred Solution: First, pay the incentive owed. A good lawyer will have no trouble in convincing a judge that the company is in breach of contract if it fails to pay. Second, redo the compensation plan to manage upside earnings. For example, use a regressive commission rate above a high sales level, or cap the earnings on any one order or account.*

Constructing Sales Representative Formula

We use the same basic mathematical formula to construct a compensation formula for sales representatives that we use for income producers.

$$\frac{\text{compensation}}{\text{performance}} = \text{payout rate}$$

Again, compensation (the target payout amount) is divided by the performance (the preferred performance to earn the target compensation) to determine payout rate—whether a commission or bonus formula.

Follow these 10 steps to construct any sales representative sales compensation formula:

- *Step 1. Identify target total cash compensation (TTCC):* Begin by identifying the target total cash compensation for the job. This amount equals the preferred earnings levels (base plus incentive payment) for achieving expected results. This amount varies from one company to another. Some organizations follow labor market practices very closely, while others rely on internal equity. Often the amount reflects a balance of competing objectives: market rates, internal equity, cost, future objectives, and past practices. While TTCC represents a single number for a job, the actual target pay levels for specific individuals will most likely vary due to differences in base salary, or even a pay range allowing for variance in the target incentive amount.

- *Step 2. Determine the pay mix of the plan:* The pay mix is the split of the target total cash compensation into two components, a base salary and a target incentive amount. The more prominent (influential) the salesperson in the buying decision of the customer, the lower the base salary. The mix is expressed as a split of 100 percent (for example, 60/40, 70/30).

- *Step 3. Establish the pay leverage of the plan:* The leverage of the plan provides the target upside outstanding earning amount for achieving exceptional sales. The leverage is expressed as a multiplier of the target incentive. The most common leverage is "3x." That is, three times the target incentive (added back to the base salary) defines the outstanding pay level for excellent performance.

- *Step 4. Calculate range of pay opportunities:* The pay opportunities reflect the application of the company's target total cash compensation, mix, and leverage. Figure 6-10 illustrates that a TTCC of $100,000 with a mix of 50/50 and a leverage of 3x would provide the following pay opportunities:

Minimum pay (base salary)	$50,000
Target total cash compensation	$100,000
Outstanding pay *	$200,000

  *($100,000 × 0.5 × 3) + $50,000 = $200,000

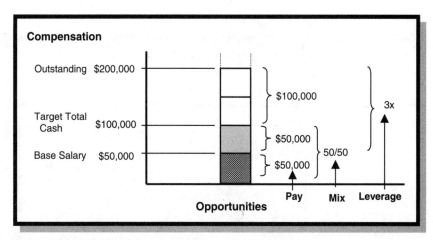

Figure 6-10. Range of Pay Opportunities

- *Step 5. Identify and weigh performance measures:* Performance measures give meaning to the sales compensation program. Performance measures are unique to the company and the job. The right performance measures will support a company's current sales objectives. Select three or fewer performance measures for the sales compensation plan. Weigh the performance measures depending on their respective importance (see Figure 6-11). Allocate target ($50,000) and outstanding incentive dollars ($100,000), depending on these weightings.

	Target Dollars	Performance Measures and Weights		
		Sales Volume (50%)	Profits (25%)	Product Mix (25%)
Minimum Incentive Pay	$0	$0	$0	$0
Target Incentive Pay	$50,000	$25,000	$12,500	$12,500
Outstanding Incentive Pay	$100,000	$50,000	$50,500	$50,500
Over Base Total Outstanding	$150,000	$75,000	$37,500	$37,500

Figure 6-11. Performance Measures and Weights

- *Step 6. Confirm quota difficulty distribution:* Make sure that quota difficulty achieves a quota distribution of a predefined percent of the sales personnel who will perform at or better than quota performance, and a percent that will perform below quota (see Figure 6-12).

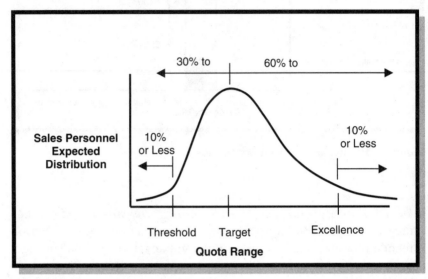

Figure 6-12. Quota Distribution

- *Step 7. Set performance expectations:* Set performance expectations for each performance measure: threshold, target, and excellence (see Figure 6-13). The summation of the performance expectations for all sales jobs should equal the business forecast.

	Performance Expectations		
Performance	**Sales Volume**	**Profits**	**New Products**
Threshold	$1,750,000	$500,000	$250,000
Target	$3,000,000	$1,000,000	$500,000
Excellence	$4,500,000	$1,500,000	$750,000

Figure 6-13. Performance Expectations

- *Step 8. Assign pay expectations with performance expectations:* Each performance level is assigned a payout amount (see Figure 6-14).

	Pay and Performance Amounts					
	Sales Volume		Profits		New Products	
	Volume	Pay	Volume	Pay	Volume	Pay
Minimum	$1,750,000	0	$500,000	0	$250,000	0
Target	$3,000,000	$25,000	$1,000,000	$12,500	$500,000	$12,500
Outstanding	$4,000,000	$50,000	$1,500,000	$25,500	$750,000	$25,000

Figure 6-14. Pay and Performance Amounts

- *Step 9. Calculate the incentive formula for each performance measure:* The incentive formula for each measure can now be calculated. Again, we use the simple formula:

$$\frac{\text{compensation}}{\text{performance}} = \text{payout rate}$$

Sales Volume Commission Rates:
1st commission rate: Threshold to target

$$\frac{\$25,000}{\$3,000,000 - \$1,750,000} \times 100 = 2\%$$

2nd commission rate: Target to excellence

$$\frac{\$50,000}{\$4,000,000 - \$3,000,000} \times 100 = 5\%$$

Profit Commission Rates:
1st commission rate: Threshold to target

$$\frac{\$12,500}{\$1,000,000 - \$500,000} \times 100 = 2.5\%$$

2nd commission rate: Target to excellence

$$\frac{\$25,000}{\$1,500,000 - \$1,000,000} \times 100 = 5.0\%$$

New Product Commission Rates:
1st commission rate:

$$\frac{\$12,500}{\$500,000 - \$250,000} \times 100 = 5\%$$

2nd commission rate:

$$\frac{\$50,000}{\$750,000 - \$500,000} \times 100 = 10\%$$

- *Step 10. Publish incentive formula:* Now the incentive formula can be published for the sales personnel (see Figure 6-15).

Component	Commission Program—3 Measures		
Base Salary	$0–(Straight Commission)		
Sales Volume Commission Rate	To Threshold Threshold to Target Over Target	**Sales Production** 0–$1,750,000 $1,750,001–$3,000,000 Over $3,000,000	**Commission Rate** 0% 2% 5%
Profit Commission Rate	To Threshold Threshold to Target Over Target	**Profit Production** 0–$500,000 $500,001–$1,000,000 Over $1,000,000	**Commission Rate** 0% 2.5% 5%
New Product Commission Rate	To Threshold Threshold to Target Over Target	**New Sales Production** 0–$250,000 $250,001–$500,000 Over $500,000	**Commission Rate** 0% 2% 5%

Figure 6-15. Commission Program

Formula Construction Worksheets

The following worksheets present a uniform method for constructing a compensation formula. These worksheets are the most popular sales compensation formulas:

1. Progressive ramp commission with base salary
2. Commission program with a multiplier and base salary
3. Bonus formula with steps
4. Bonus formula rate
5. Bonus formula matrix

Worksheet 1: Progressive Ramp Commission with Base Salary

This sales compensation formula pays commission on all sales (see Figures 6-16 and 6-17). The commission rate has a progressive ramp and is uncapped. There is no threshold. Performance is 100 percent of sales volume. The plan provides a single base salary level for all job incumbents.

	Steps	Formula Parameters		
1	Total Target Compensation	$95,000		
2	Pay Mix	70/30		
3	Leverage	3x		
4	Pay Opportunities	Base Salary:	$66,500 ($95,000 x .70 = $66,500)	
		Target Incentive:	$28,500 ($95,000 x .30 = $28,500)	
		Outstanding Pay:	$152,000 ($28,500 x 3 + $66,500 = $152,000)	
5	Measures and Weights	Sales Volume:	100%	
6	Quota Distribution	Meet/Exceed Target:	60%–70%	
		Below Target:	30%–40%	
7	Performance Expectations	Threshold:	$0	
		Target Performance:	$1,000,000	
		Excellence:	$2,000,000	
8	Assign Pay Opportunities to Performance Expectations		Performance Levels	Pay Opportunities
		Threshold:	$0	$66,500 (Base Salary)
		Target:	$1,000,000	$28,500 (Target Pay)
		Excellence:	$2,000,000	$57,000 (Outstanding Pay)
9	Calculate Formula	1st Commission Rate $$\frac{\$28,500}{\$3,000,000} \times 100 = 2.85\%$$ 2nd Commission Rate $$\frac{\$152,000-\$95,000}{2,000,000-\$1,000,000} \times 100 = 5.7\%$$		
10	Publish Formula	Sales Volume Production	Commission Rate	
		0–1,000,0000	2.85%	
		Over 1,000,000	5.70%	

Figure 6-16. Worksheet #1—Progressive ramp commission with base salary

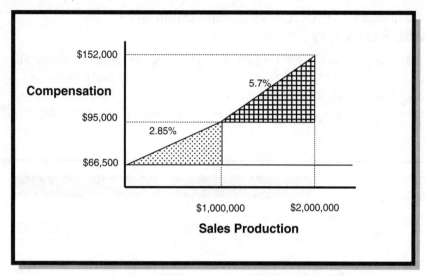

Figure 6-17. Progressive Ramp Commission with Base Salary

Worksheet 2: Commission Program with a Multiplier and Base Salary

This sales compensation plan has a base salary range and a commission on all sales, with no threshold (see Figure 6-18). There are two measures: sales volume and gross margin. Gross margin is a linked multiplier measure that increases or decreases the value of the sales volume commission based on gross margin performance. Sales volume is weighted 70 percent in the plan; gross margin is weighted 30 percent.

	Steps	Formula Parameters		
1	Total Target Compensation	$60,000		
2	Pay Mix	75/25		
3	Leverage	3x		
4	Pay Opportunities	**Base Salary Range**		
		Minimum:	$36,000 ($45,000 x .80 = $36,000)	
		Midpoint:	$45,000 ($60,000 x .75 = $45,000)	
		Maximum:	$54,000 ($45,000 x 1.2 = $54,000)	
		Target Base Salary:	$45,000 (75% of $60,000)	
		Target Incentive:	$15,000 (25% of $60,000)	
		Outstanding Pay:	$90,000 (($15,000 x 3 + $45,000)= $90,000)	
5	Measures and Weights	Sales Volume: 70%	$10,500 ($15,000 x .70= $10,500)	
		Gross Margin Percent: 30%	$ 4,500 ($15,000 x .30 = $4,500)	
6	Quota Distribution	Meet/Exceed Target: 60%–70%		
		Below Target: 30%–40%		
7	Performance Expectations	**Performance Range**		
			Revenue	Gross Margin Percent
		Threshold:	$ 0	23%
		Target Performance:	$750,000	26%
		Excellence Performance:	$1,500,000	31%
8	Assign Pay Opportunities to Performance Expectations	**Total Pay Opportunity**		
			Components	Cumulative
		Threshold:	$45,000 (Base Salary)	$45,000
		Target Incentive:	$15,000	$60,000
		Excellence:	$30,000 (Outstanding Pay)	$90,000
		Pay Components by Performance Measure		
			Sales Volume	Gross Margin
			Result Pay	Result Multiple
		Threshold:	0 0	23% ($4,500)*
		Target:	$750,000 $15,000	26% $0
		Excellence:	$1,500,000 $21,000	31% $9,000
		*$4,500 is potential monies at risk for performing between 23% and 26% gross margin. Amount to be deducted from sales volume commission dollars.		

Figure 6-18. Worksheet #2—Commission program with a multiplier and base salary

9	Calculate Formula	**Sales Volume Commission Rates**

1st Commission Rate

$$\frac{\$15,000}{\$750,000} \times 100 = 2.0\%$$

2nd Commission Rate

$$\frac{\$21,000 - \$15,000}{\$1,000,000 - \$750,000} \times 100 = 3.6\%$$

thus,

$$\frac{\$9,000}{\$250,000} \times 100 = 3.6\%$$

Multiplier

To calculate the multiplier, determine the percent available for each percent of gross margin achieved:

The **take-away** multiplier for below-target performance:

$$\frac{(\$4,500)/\$15,000}{26 - 23} = (.10)$$

The **additive** multiplier rate for each percent of gross margin performance for above-target performance:

$$\frac{\$9,000/\$21,000}{31 - 26} = .086$$

The schedule for the multiplier is as follows:

Gross Margin	Rate	Multiplier of Commission Dollars
23%	(.10%)	70%
24%	(.10%)	80%
25%	(.10%)	90%
26%	0%	100%
27%	0.086	108.6%
28%	0.086	117.2%
29%	0.086	125.8%
30%	0.086	134.4%
31%	0.086	143.0%

Figure 6-18. *(Continued)*

10	Publish Formula	Base Salary Range:

Base Salary Range:

Minimum	Midpoint	Maximum
$36,0000	$45,000	$54,0000

Sales Volume Commission Formula

Sales Volume Production	Commission Rate
0–$750,000	0%
$750,001–$1,000,000	2.0%
Over $1,000,000	3.6%

Gross Margin Multiplier (Percent of Commission Dollars)

Gross Margin	Multiplier
23%	70%
24%	80%
25%	90%
26%	100%
27%	108.6%
28%	117.2%
29%	125.8%
30%	134.4%
31%	143.0%

Figure 6-18. *(Continued)*

Worksheet 3: Bonus Formula with Steps

Worksheet 3 (see Figure 6-19) shows how to calculate a bonus formula with steps, a base salary, and a performance threshold.

	Steps	Formula Parameters	
1	Total Target Compensation	$100,000	
2	Pay Mix	75/25	
3	Leverage	3x	
4	Pay Opportunities	**Base Salary Range**	
		Minimum:	$60,000 ($75,000 x .8 = $60,000)
		Midpoint:	$75,000 ($100,000 x .75 = $75,000)
		Maximum:	$90,000 ($75,000 x 1.2 = $90,000)
		Target Base Salary:	$75,000 ($100,000 x .75 = $75,000)
		Target Incentive:	$25,000 ($100,000 x .25 = $25,000)
		Outstanding Pay:	150,000 ($25,000 x 3 + $75,000 = $150,000)
5	Measures and Weights	Sales Volume:	100%
6	Quota Distribution	Meet/Exceed Target: 60%–70%	
		Below Target: 30%–40%	
7	Performance Expectations	**Performance Range**	
			Percent to Goal Revenue
		Threshold:	50%
		Target Performance:	100%
		Excellence Performance:	130%

8	Assign Pay Opportunities to Performance Expectations	**Total Pay Opportunity**		
			Components	Cumulative
		Threshold:	$75,000 (base salary)	$75,000
		Target Incentive:	$25,000	$100,000
		Excellence:	$50,000 (outstanding Pay)	$150,000

Pay Compensation By Performance Measure

Sales Volume

	Result*	Pay
Minimum:	60%	$5,000
Target:	100%	$25,000
Outstanding:	130%	$50,000

*Sales results are expressed as a percent of quota performance

Figure 6-19. Worksheet #3: Bonus Formula with Steps

9	Calculate Formula	**Bonus Formula Payout Steps**

Calculate payout in four steps of 10% increments.
Express payout as a percent of target incentive ($25,000)

To calculate the bonus formula steps, determine the value of each step for below-quota performance and then for above-quota performance.

Below-quota performance: Calculate the steps for below target performance:

$$\frac{(\$25,000)/\$25,000}{(100-50)/10} = .20$$

Above-quota performance: Calculate the steps for above target performance.

$$\frac{\$50,000/\$25,000}{(140-100)/10} = .50$$

The schedule for the steps is as follows:

Percent Quota	Rate	Percent of Target Incentive
50%	.0	0%
60%	.20	20%
70%	.20	40%
80%	.20	60%
90%	.20	80%
100%	.20	100.0%
110%	.50	150.0%
120%	.50	200.0%
130%	.50	250.0%
140%	.50	300.0%

10	Publish Formula	**Base Salary Range**

Minimum	Midpoint	Maximum
$60,0000	$75,000	$90,0000

Bonus Steps
Paid as a percent of target incentive

Percent to Quota	Percent of Target Incentive
50%	0%
60%	20%
70%	40%
80%	60%
90%	80%
100%	100.0%
110%	150.0%
120%	200.0%
130%	250.0%
140%	300.0%

Figure 6-19. *(Continued)*

Worksheet 4: Bonus Formula Rate

This bonus formula rate (see Figures 6-20 and 6-21) provides payouts for each percent of quota performance. The plan has a base salary and a performance threshold. Bonus rate is expressed as a percent of salary range midpoint. Use bonus formula rate when performance range is narrow and each percent of quota is significant. As a bonus formula, dissimilar-sized territories are "made equal" for compensation purposes by tying payouts to percent of quota performance, regardless of actual quota volume.

	Steps	Formula Parameters		
1	Total Target Compensation	$80,000		
2	Pay Mix	80/20		
3	Leverage	3x		
4	Pay Opportunities	**Base Salary Range**		
		Minimum:	$51,200 ($64,000 x .8 = $51,200)	
		Midpoint:	$64,000 ($80,000 x .8 = $64,000)	
		Maximum:	$78,000 ($64,000 x 1.2 = $78,000)	
		Target Base Salary:	$64,000 ($80,000 x .80 = $64,000)	
		Target Incentive:	$16,000 ($80,000 x .20 = $16,000)	
		Outstanding Pay:	$112,000 ($16,000 x 3 + $64,000 = $112,000)	
5	Measures and Weights	Sales Volume:	100%	
6	Quota Distribution	Meet/Exceed Target:	60%–70%	
		Below Target:	30%–40%	
7	Performance Expectations	**Performance Range**	Percent to Goal Revenue	
		Threshold:	75%	
		Target Performance:	100%	
		Excellence Performance:	125%	
8	Assign Pay Opportunities to Performance Expectations	**Total Pay Opportunity**		
			Components	Cumulative
		Threshold:	$64,000 (Base Salary)	$64,000
		Target Incentive:	$16,000	$80,000
		Excellence:	$32,000 (Outstanding Pay)	$112,000
		Pay Compensation by Performance Measure		
			Sales Volume Result*	Pay
		Minimum:	75%	$0
		Target:	100%	$16,000
		Outstanding:	125%	$48,000
		*Sales results are expressed as a percent of quota performance		

Figure 6-20. Worksheet #4: Bonus Formula Rate

9	Calculate Formula	**Bonus Formula Payout Rate**
		Express payout as a percent of salary range midpoint ($64,000)
		To calculate the bonus formula rate, determine the value of each percent for below-quota performance and then for above-quota performance.
		<u>Below-Quota Performance.</u> Calculate the payout rate for below-target performance:
		$$\frac{(\$80,000-\$64,000)/\$64,000}{(100-75)} \times 100 = 1\%$$
		<u>Above-Quota Performance.</u> Calculate the above-quota performance payout rate:
		$$\frac{(\$112,000-\$80,000)/\$64,000}{(125-100)} \times 100 = 2\%$$
10	Publish Formula	**Base Salary Range**
		<div>Minimum Midpoint Maximum $60,000 $75,000 $90,000</div>
		Bonus Rate
		For Each Pay a Percent to Percent of <u>Quota</u> <u>Base Midpoint</u> 0 – 74% 0 75 – 100% 1% Over 100% 2%

Figure 6-20. *(Continued)*

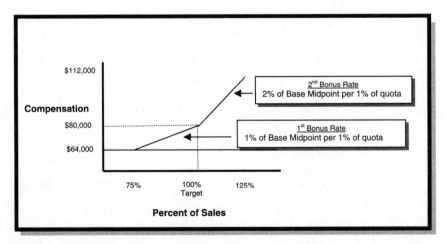

Figure 6-21. Bonus Formula Rate

Worksheet 5: Bonus Formula Matrix

Use a bonus formula matrix when territories are dissimilar in size and the salesperson must resolve objectives on two competing measures (see Figure 6-22).

	Steps		Formula Parameters		
1	Total Target Compensation		$120,000		
2	Pay Mix		70/30		
3	Leverage		3x		
4	Pay Opportunities	Base Salary Range			
		Minimum:	$67,200 ($84,000 x .8 = $67,200)		
		Midpoint:	$84,000 (120,000 x .7 = $84,000)		
		Maximum:	$100,800 ($84,000 x 1.2 = $100,800)		
		Target Base Salary:	$84,000 ($120,000 x .7 = $84,000)		
		Target Incentive:	$36,000 ($120,000 x .3 = $36,000)		
		Outstanding Pay:	$192,000 ($36,000 x 3 + $84,000)		
5	Measures and Weights	Sales Volume:	50%		
		Price Realization:	50%		
6	Quota Distribution	Meet/Exceed Target:	60%–70%		
		Below Target:	30%–40%		
7	Performance Expectations	Performance Range			
			Percent to Goal Revenue		Price Realization
		Threshold:	60%		92%
		Target Performance:	100%		100%
		Excellence Performance:	140%		108%
8	Assign Pay Opportunities to Performance Expectations	Total Pay Opportunity			
			Components		Cumulative
		Threshold:	$84,000 (Base Salary)		$84,000
		Target Incentive:	$36,000		$36,000
		Excellence:	$72,000 (Outstanding Pay)		$192,000
		Pay Compensation by Performance Measure			
			Sales Volume		Price Realization
			Result* Pay		Result Pay
		Minimum:	60% $0		92% 0
		Target:	100% $18,000		100% $18,000
		Outstanding:	125% $36,000		110% $36,000
		*Sales results are expressed as a percent of quota performance			

Figure 6-22. Worksheet #5: Bonus Formula Matrix

9	Calculate Formula	**Bonus Formula Matrix**

Establish the number of rows and columns

9 rows by 9 columns

Determine "penalty" for achieving one goal without achieving the other:

40% loss of target bonus for revenue and price realization

Set the corners

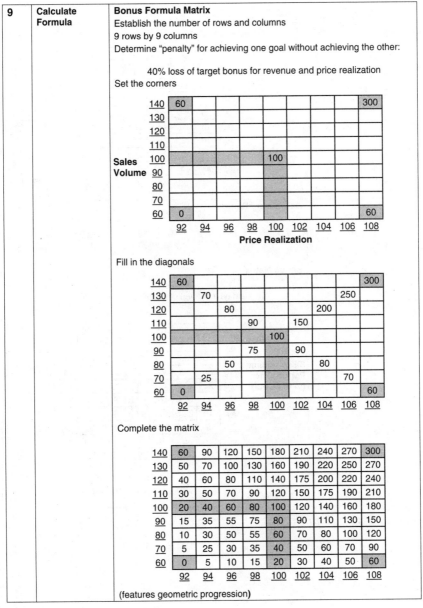

Fill in the diagonals

Complete the matrix

(features geometric progression)

Figure 6-22. *(Continued)*

Or, calculate bonus matrix with nonlinear slopes

	92	94	96	98	100	102	104	106	108
140	60	80	100	120	140	180	220	260	300
130	50	70	90	110	130	162.5	195	227.5	260
120	40	60	80	100	120	145	170	195	220
110	30	50	70	90	110	127.5	145	162.5	180
100	20	40	60	80	100	110	120	130	140
90	15	31.3	47.5	63.8	80	90	100	110	120
80	10	22.5	35.0	47.5	60	70	80	90	100
70	5	13.8	22.5	31.3	40	50	60	70	80
60	0	5	10	15	20	30	40	50	60

10	Publish Formula

Base Salary Range

Minimum	Midpoint	Maximum
$67,200	$84,000	$100,800

Bonus Matrix

Paid as a percent of target incentive = $36,000

Sales Volume Performance (% to Quota)

	92	94	96	98	100	102	104	106	108
140	60	80	100	120	140	180	220	260	300
130	50	70	90	110	130	162.5	195	227.5	260
120	40	60	80	100	120	145	170	195	220
110	30	50	70	90	110	127.5	145	162.5	180
100	20	40	60	80	100	110	120	130	140
90	15	31.3	47.5	63.8	80	90	100	110	120
80	10	22.5	35.0	47.5	60	70	80	90	100
70	5	13.8	22.5	31.3	40	50	60	70	80
60	0	5	10	15	20	30	40	50	60

Price Realization (% to Quota)

Figure 6-22. *(Continued)*

Summary

The math is simple. Income producers get a percent of what they sell. Determine the preferred cost of sales and make that the commission rate. For sales representatives, determine what you want sales personnel to earn and how much volume they should produce, then simply divide pay by performance to get the payout rate.

7

Support Programs: Territories, Quotas, and Crediting

Sales compensation programs function in concert with the following support programs: territory configuration, quota management, and sales crediting. Each of these mission-critical support programs performs an important sales management role. Collectively, sales compensation and these support programs form the backbone of the sales performance management system. Sales management needs to continually define, monitor, and revise these support programs to serve the company's evolving sales strategy. The success of the sales compensation program rests with the effectiveness of these interdependent programs. Consequently, when redesigning the sales compensation program, sales management must also review and revise these support programs.

Briefly, each of these support programs can affect the sales compensation program including scope of responsibilities, performance commitment, and achievement measurement in the following manner:

- *Territory configuration:* Territory configuration defines sales territories—"scope of responsibilities." The territory configuration policies provide rules for account assignment and reassignment.

- *Quota management:* Quotas define performance expectations— "performance commitment." Quota management encompasses two activities: quota allocation and quota adjustments.

- *Sales crediting:* Sales crediting defines sales success—"achievement measurement." Sales crediting specifies to whom and when individuals earn sales credit for compensation purposes.

The material that follows examines territory, quota, and sales crediting practices for sales representatives, but not for income producers. While some of these concepts do apply to income producers, they

have a more limited application. So, our focus is on sales representatives—those who can earn and exceed a target incentive for sales
performance.

Territory Configuration

Sales management assigns accounts to territories for sales coverage
purposes. The best performing sales organizations structure territories with homogeneous buyer populations making it easier for sales
personnel to identify customer needs, deliver sales messages, and
guide customer decision-making.

Because sales personnel receive incentive compensation payments
for territory sales performance, we will examine how initial territory
configuration and account reassignment practices affect sales compensation effectiveness. We will begin with a review of the most
prevalent territory types. Then we will examine practices for making
account changes mid-year, an area that needs watchful governance.

Configuring Effective Sales Territories

The art of configuring effective sales territories requires superior interpretation of company business strategy, rigorous analytical investigation, and studied judgment about customer needs. The objective of
effective territory design is clear: create sales territories with the best
return on sales investment dollars. This means optimizing dozens of
trade-offs to arrive at the optimal territory design so that profitable
revenue production is high and sales costs are low. Some sales organizations invest substantial resources in gathering market information
and performance yield data to construct advanced analytical-based
territory optimization models. Others find the variables so complex or
resources so limited; they make their best guesstimate of the right territories and then make real-time adjustments as performance unfolds.
Finally, others maintain historical territories as a rational approach if
business conditions remain unchanged, but this is a risky position
when sales conditions *are* changing.

For sales representative jobs, sales management attempts to provide
balanced (equally challenging) territories by using different job titles.
In this manner, sales management seeks to configure territories of

equal opportunity so incumbents have an equal chance to earn and exceed the target pay for the job. In an ideal world, the sales territories would be equal on the following factors:

- Number and revenue of existing customers
- Number and revenue of potential new customers
- Amount of available selling time
- Extent of customer needs
- Customer accessibility: travel distance, sales access time

Of course, it's impossible to configure sales territories to create truly equal sales opportunities. There are just too many variables. Sales organizations generally attempt, as best they can, to provide balance to the selling opportunity through effective territory configuration.

Although territory balance is important, focus is more important. Sales organizations need to focus sales personnel to optimize the learning process and selling time. For this reason, sales organizations seeking focus and hoping for balance will configure territories using one or more of the following criteria:

- *Geography:* One of the most popular methods of organizing salespeople is by geographic area. Geographic territories assume the buyers are alike and one salesperson can handle all the customers within a geographic area.

- *Stratified/size:* Another method of organizing territories is by account size. In a stratified sales organization, one group of salespeople calls on large customers; another group calls on medium-sized customers; and a low-cost resource handles small customers. A stratified sales organization will most likely have both named-account and geographic territories.

- *Account status:* Another territory configuration method divides territories into two categories: noncustomers and existing customers. Sometimes called "hunter and farmer" territories, this configuration allows sales personnel to focus on one primary task: hunters who sell to new accounts and farmers who manage existing accounts.

- *Vertical/industry:* Grouping accounts by industry type (vertical) provides sales personnel with the ability to understand the unique buying needs of a group of similar customers. Examples of vertical/industry territories include financial services, telecommunications, and consumer packaged goods.

- *Product/application:* Another territory configuration method groups current and target customers into territories based on product or user application. These types of territories place a premium on sales personnel product or application knowledge.

- *Project opportunity territories:* Some types of selling are opportunistic and are based on customer projects. Instead of a defined, ongoing territory of accounts, sales management assigns these sales opportunities to sales personnel as they arise. Examples include selling equipment and services to support major construction and engineering projects. Sales management defines the territories as a summation of these assigned major projects.

- *Hybrid:* Many sales organizations use a mix of territory types, even blending one or more together to achieve optimal sales coverage.

Optimal territory configuration uses sales resources efficiently. From a sales compensation perspective, effective territory configuration provides equal sales opportunities to all sales personnel in the same job. While this does not mean identical sales opportunity, it does accommodate the less exacting objective of comparable sales opportunity. *Comparable* means sales personnel view the sales challenge among territories to have relative trade-offs, and sales personnel in one territory are not significantly advantaged or disadvantaged by territory configuration.

Vocabulary Alert: "Geographic" and "named" account territories often coexist. Geographic defines territories in spatial terms such as region, state, county, zip codes, or manager-defined boundaries. Named-account territories define territories as a list of accounts. These two terms, used together, provide ample descriptive context. For example, "Your territory includes all accounts with the following zip codes . . ." or "Your territory is this list of major accounts . . ." or "Your territory includes five counties in western Pennsylvania, less the named major accounts." Or lastly, "Your territory includes all major named accounts in Illinois."

Mid-Year Sales Territory Changes

Territory reconfiguration usually takes place at the start of the fiscal year along with the assignment of new quotas and the introduction of new sales compensation plans. Sales management, during this time, makes every effort to bring balance to the sales territories in order to optimize the return on sales resource investment. However, there are numerous occasions mid-year when sales management needs to reconfigure sales territories. These mid-year changes to territories can impact the entire sales force or occur on a case-by-case basis. Adding or removing accounts from a territory will most likely increase or decrease payouts. Minor changes in pay opportunity—either up or down—may be acceptable without making pay program adjustments. Sales management must provide explicit policies for addressing mid-year territory changes whether they occur on an across-the-board basis or as one-off changes.

Mid-year territory changes can occur because of a variety of practical business issues:

- *Strategic focus change:* A company may require a reconfiguration of territories if the strategic focus changes regarding products or customers.

- *Staffing changes:* Changes in staffing levels, either increases or decreases, will affect sales territory definition. These changes may be caused by economic prospects, either positive or negative, or by mergers and acquisitions.

- *Customer changes:* Customer openings, relocations, and closures will change the census of customers within a territory.

- *Customer request:* Occasionally, customers may request a change in sales personnel (not a high vote of confidence for the salesperson).

- *Temporary changes:* When sales personnel are terminated or when a salesperson cannot cover his or her accounts because of vacation, illness, or temporary assignment, others may be asked to temporarily assume account responsibilities.

Sales Compensation Policies and Territory Changes

Sales management should strive to avoid mid-year changes to the compensation plan. However, in some cases where major territory changes occur, sales management will need to make adjustments.

The following are sample policies for mid-year territory changes.

- *"No changes will be made to the compensation program or quotas if the territory changes affect less than 15% of the performance opportunity."*

- *"There is no retention of any historical sales or revenue credit when an account moves from one territory to another. In no case will two sales personnel receive credit for the same account."* (See Sales Crediting, starting at the bottom of p. 145.)

- *"For target incentive commission plans, if the territory changes affect more than 15% of the performance opportunity, declines of greater than 15% will be protected with a guaranteed minimum payment. If performance opportunity increases greater than 15%, the dollar amount where progressive ramps increase will be adjusted upward by the estimated percent of performance opportunity expansion."*

- *"For target incentive bonus plans, if the territory changes affect more than 15% of the performance opportunity, the quotas will be adjusted to match the expected increase or decrease in performance opportunity."*

Precluding Account Reconfiguration Abuses

In rare cases, unscrupulous sales personnel, sometimes in collusion with sales management, can manipulate the account assignment practices to inflate earnings. The sales compensation program should have a clear statement of consequence for any type of manipulation of the compensation program at the expense of the company.

Sales management should monitor the account assignment practices for the following types of abuses:

- *Quota relief:* Removing an account from a territory, in some companies, automatically lowers the quota. This technique is applicable when a customer's status changes, such as when a facility closes. However, a dishonest practice removes the account from the territory not because of legitimate customer status changes, but because sales performance for the account is so poor. The salesperson gets a free ride by having the quota reduced for poor performance.

- *Upside benefit:* In another twist, assignment of an account to a territory to benefit a sales representative without increasing the quota is another form of manipulation. Local sales managers sometimes assign such accounts temporarily or permanently to a sales person allowing higher pay to be earned against the (incorrectly) unadjusted quota.

It is best to keep mid-year account changes to a minimum. Any account assignment changes should have several levels of approval. All such changes should be visible and available on regular monthly reports showing the extent and impact of account changes by person for the period (monthly or quarterly) and the cumulative impact on the company on a year-to-date basis.

Quota Management

Quota management includes two components: quota allocation and quota adjustments. As with account configuration, quota allocation—the establishment of individual quotas—should occur at the start of the fiscal year. There are numerous techniques for allocating quotas, and we will examine several of the more popular methods. Quota adjustments occur during the year and for numerous reasons. We will look at these instances and provide guidance on how to address mid-year quota changes.

How Quotas Affect Sales Compensation

The impact of quotas varies depending on the type of sales compensation plan. For income producers with a flat commission, a quota might be merely a symbolic point, marking expected performance but without any financial impact. Also, quotas might be a point where the commission rate changes or is an important milestone affecting the relationship between the income producer and the company.

Quotas play a more important role for sales representatives as compared to income producers. Sales management uses quotas to distribute the corporate sales commitment to all sales personnel. For these target incentive plans, both commission and bonus formula, the target quota defines the degree of difficulty where two-thirds of sales personnel will exceed this number and one-third will not. For formulas with ramps (progressive or regressive), the quota will provide one of the break-points where the formula rate changes.

For target incentive commission plans, the average territory quota provides the calculation basis for establishing the commission rate. For target bonus incentive plans, quotas play a pivotal role in equalizing the earning potential of dissimilar-sized territories. Additionally, in target bonus plans, the quota is an integral part of the payout formula. For this reason, quotas must be accurate—if they are too easy, the plan will overpay; if the quotas are too difficult, the plan will underpay.

Vocabulary Alert: Companies use words like *forecast, plan, goal,* and *quota* differently. However, in all cases, these words describe objective-based numbers. In some companies, management uses these words interchangeably; in other companies, each of these words has a specific meaning. However, most companies use *forecast* and *plan* (a noun, as in the business plan) to describe a companywide commitment. "The forecast for the coming fiscal year is to hit $875M in sales." Or "Our plan is to achieve $875M in sales." On the other hand, both *goal* and *quota* usually describe performance objectives for individuals or sales teams. "Your quota for your territory is $2.6M." Sales forecasting establishes a company's overall sales objective and quota allocation distributes the forecast to sales personnel as individual quotas.

Quota Allocation

Companies have numerous quota allocation methods to distribute the company's forecast to sales personnel. Quota allocation methods feature a combination of analytical tools and process methods. Regarding analytics, some quota allocation methods make scant use of market potential data and simply use last year's performance as the basis of this year's quota. Others invest significantly in measuring territory potential, territory market share, account growth rates, and account intelligence to create advanced analytical models for allocating quotas. From a process perspective, similar extremes exist. In some companies, sales personnel are not involved in the quota allocation process and simply receive an assigned quota number. In other companies, extensive field involvement in the quota allocation process includes active participation of sales personnel and field sales management. The most popular quota allocation methods are as follows:

- *Top down/algorithm:* For industries where the product sales growth is tied to economic cycles and there are numerous customers (too many to know individual buying practices), the top down/algorithm method is the best quota allocation method. Management uses historical data and economic projections to create a mathematical model, an algorithm, to allocate quotas.

- *Top down/negotiated allocation:* Another method brings organization peers together to negotiate quota allocation decisions. The vice president (VP) of sales meets with his or her regional managers (RM) to allocate the VP's quota among the RMs. Regional managers then meet with their respective direct reports, the district managers (DMs). Working with the district managers, the RM then allocates his or her number among the DMs and the process continues down the organizational chart until the process fully allocates all the forecast to individual sales personnel.

- *Top down, bottom up:* A third method features parallel activities of top-down quota allocation and bottom-up quota estimates. This process creates two quota allocation views. A reconciliation process at each level helps align these two quota allocation estimates.

- *Account planning:* Territories composed of a few large accounts use account planning methods to set quotas. Major account sales personnel are the best qualified to help construct a sales estimate for their large customers. Assembling a customer business plan, the major account manager presents this sales estimate to senior sales management for review and adjustments. The outcome of this planning and review process produces a quota for the large named-account territory.

Most companies need to use a combination of quota-setting methods to fully allocate the company forecast.

Hands-Free Quotas. An alternate method to assigning quotas is not to assign quotas. Known as "hands-free" quotas, no attempt is made to make individual quota allocation assignment. Instead, actual sales performance creates a percentile rank-order of the sales personnel. A formula provides payouts of the target incentive amount depending on percentile ranking. In this manner, there are no quotas. However, this approach has several noteworthy shortcomings. First, sales management compromises its leadership charter by not providing a meaningful performance goal for the organization and for individuals. Second, individual sales personnel have no idea how they are performing until after the ranking. They must wait for their individual percentile ranking. Lastly, it creates an internally competitive atmosphere where sales personnel knowingly compete against one another.

Special Issues in Quota Allocation

The following present special challenges to quota allocation:

- *Over-assignment/under-assignment:* Some sales management teams intentionally over-assign or under-assign the forecast during the quota allocation process. Over-assignment occurs when the summation of individual quotas exceeds the overall forecast objective. Sales leaders who advocate this practice believe the extra cushion helps ensure that the sales team will make its number, given unexpected events such as customer changes, product issues, or turnover among sales personnel. Under-assignment, sometimes known as breakage, is the opposite of over-assignment. Sales leaders do not fully allocate the forecast. There are numerous reasons for this practice. The most common is to protect sales personnel from an unrealistic forecast created by corporate management. Another reason is to avoid the uncertainty of placing large unpredictable orders into individual quotas. In such cases, these uncertain large orders remain outside the individual quotas, but are often assigned to a sales manager.

    For whatever reason, when sales leaders choose to over-assign or under-assign quotas, they run the risk of eroding their credibility or the credibility of the quota allocation process. At a certain point, sales personnel will learn that their quotas are not true quotas and therefore are open for adjustments, challenges and compromise.

- *Seasonality:* Some sales cycles are very seasonal, peaking at different times of the year. If performance and pay periods align with these seasonal fluctuations, then sales management needs to assign seasonally adjusted quotas.

- *Market uncertainty:* Market uncertainty—potential high growth or significant declines—makes quota allocation more problematic. Two potential solutions exist: shorten the performance period or use rolling averages. If sales management does not have the market visibility to set realistic one-year quotas, then shortening the performance period for quotas can help. Instead of 12-month quotas, set 6-month quotas, or even quarterly quotas. Another method is to use a rolling-average quota calculated by taking the last 3 months of actual performance multiplied by an adjustment factor (plus or minus) to calculate the next performance period quota.

- *Long sales cycles:* Long sales cycles present another challenge for quota allocation. When the sales cycle is greater than 12 months, annual quotas become irrelevant. In such cases, it's best to move to an event-based incentive plan where payouts are tied to sales events such as contract signing and not quota performance.

- *Periodic mega orders:* Some sales models have a mix of predictable sales orders interspersed with unpredictable mega (large) orders. It's best not to place these mega orders into the quota; instead, provide a separate payout formula for these orders, correctly applying a regressive rate above a certain dollar volume. This separate schedule is further enhanced by requiring sales personnel to register major deals. Without preregistering a deal, the incentive compensation available for such orders is significantly lower. This policy supports the following rationale: "If you had no knowledge of the order, then you did not have much influence on the purchase . . . ; therefore, your pay should be commensurate with your degree of influence . . . which shouldn't be much."

- *New products:* At the beginning of each fiscal year, product management may have a schedule of new product launches. Predicting with accuracy the launch of these new products affects the quota allocation process. If the launch dates are accurate and the sales performance expectations realistic, then sales management should include these new products in the quota. However, if the dates are not confirmed or the projected sales volumes are indeterminate, then exclude these new products from the quota. Give them their own launch incentive (an add-on) that expires at the end of the performance period. Then, when you have more solid information, include these new products in the quota for the next performance period.

Quota allocation provides sales leadership with an opportunity to manage performance. Quota allocation requires ongoing efforts from year to year to make adjustments and improvements.

Mid-Year Quota Changes

Most companies need to consider mid-year changes to quotas. Like mid-year account changes, mid-year quota changes require across-the-board adjustments, or case-by-case changes. Sales management seeks to balance quota fairness by achieving forecast commitment. While some mid-year changes cause an increase in quotas, many petitions for mid-year changes are the opposite, causing a reduction in quotas—with no commensurate reduction in earning opportunities.

Complex sales organizations often provide for mid-year changes, but limit the scope of such changes with restrictive policies such as the following:

- *"No quota change can be made unless the performance opportunity will be altered by greater than 15%."*

- *"Quota adjustments are considered for changes outside the influence of the salesperson, but excludes activities associated with customer-buying practices, market trends, competitor actions, company fulfillment, and company terms policies."*

- *"No quota adjustments can be made without commensurate adjustments to other quotas to offset the change, positive or negative."*

- *"Any quota adjustment must be approved by all regional managers, the chief financial officer (CFO), and the vice president of sales."*

- *"No quota adjustments can be applied retroactively and none can be made at any other time than the beginning of the fiscal quarter."*

While most companies will need to make quota adjustments, restricting quota changes enhances the importance of the quota and precludes excessive requests for dubious quota adjustments.

Making Mid-Year Changes

In some cases, sales management will need to make mid-year quota changes. The following are compelling reasons to make mid-year changes:

- *Major economic change:* Whether a dramatic positive upswing or a profound downswing in the economy, sales management may need to adjust quotas. For major changes in the economy, an across-the-board quota increase will recalibrate performance and payout expectations. A best-practice technique is to terminate the current plan, make all legally obligated payments under the current plan, then begin a new plan with the appropriate adjustments.

- *Account changes:* Whether caused by mergers, acquisitions, reorganization, or account assignment fine tuning, make quota adjustments if the changes affect the performance opportunity by more than 15 percent.

- *Currency and pricing changes:* Changes in revenue value caused by currency fluctuations or company pricing decisions should cause a similar offsetting adjustment to quotas.

- *Acts of God:* Most sales compensation plans allow for quota adjustments caused by acts of God, such as major weather calamities.

In summary, some quota adjustments may be necessary, but restrict the practice to protect the integrity of the quota management process.

Sales Crediting

Sales crediting specifies when sales personnel earn credit for a sale. We will examine sales crediting eligibility, timing, and adjustments.

Sales Credit Eligibility

Who should get credit for a sale? The answer should be simple: the salesperson—the person who closed the sale . . . right? In sales organizations with a single sales force, applying this eligibility definition is relatively easy. However, in more complex sales organizations with multiple channels, overlay sales specialists, and team selling, the definition of sales credit eligibility becomes more clouded.

There are three major categories of sales crediting:

- *Seller sales credit:* Simplify sales crediting by assigning it to those who have customer contact and can persuade the customer to act. The single seller who influenced the customer to buy should receive 100 percent of the sales credit. If two or more sellers influence the customer, then those sellers share the sales credit using a prespecified proportional split. In target-incentive bonus formula design, sales management can double credit both sellers, but each seller must have an identical up-lift in their quotas to offset the double crediting. In this manner, while sales crediting is double counted, it does not elevate payouts.

- *Vertical sales credit:* Vertical sales credit refers to the upward crediting of sales results through the field management layers. This is an acceptable accounting recognition practice. This is legitimate and is not considered to be double crediting.

- *Horizontal sales credit:* Horizontal sales credit provides sales credit to resources who are not the primary sellers. In a true economic sense, this form of sales crediting generates additional double costs. Sales management often uses this form of double crediting to support the field sales strategy. Sales credit is often awarded to sales support resources such as product overlay specialists and presales support personnel. For example, a regional product overlay specialist will earn sales credit for all sales in the region regardless of his or her involvement with a specific sale. Presales support specialists provide another example where double sales crediting supports the overall sales strategy. In both cases, sales management makes a conscious decision to reward more than one person for a sale. In these examples, horizontal sales credit promotes cooperation between sales personnel and those assigned to support them in the sales process.

Well-crafted policies regarding sales crediting eligibility will suppress some of the following sales crediting errors:

- *Landlording:* Sales personnel do not own accounts and therefore receive automatic sales credit for all products sold to the customer. Some sales might come from another sales channel independent of the salesperson. In such situations, sales personnel do not earn credit (as a landlord) on those sales, specifically sales they did not influence.

- *Appeasement pay:* Sales management will want the field organization to support a new channel, such as the telephone sales personnel. In an attempt to win the support from the existing direct sales channel, sales management incorrectly double credits both parties.

- *Annuity business:* The general rule is to "pay for persuasion once." Providing ongoing sales credit to sales from previous years, now covered by a contract and managed by the customer service department, is an ineffective use of incentive dollars.

Sales Credit Timing

Sales credit timing specifies when sales management recognizes a sale for incentive credit purposes. There are several points in the sales/purchase process where this credit can occur. Assign earned sales credit to the salesperson at the point where the customer purchase is assured because you want the salesperson to stop thinking about the order. There are several points along the purchase continuum where sales management can recognize sales credit:

- *Product specification:* Certain industries recognize sales prior to a sales event. In purchasing components for their product, a customer will specify a vendor's product. Examples include design-wins for semiconductor sales or building materials specification for funded major commercial projects. Even though the customer has not issued a formal purchase order, the specification confirms that the order will be forthcoming. Some sales organizations accept specification for sales crediting purposes.

- *Booking:* An order is booked when a company accepts an order. Many sales organizations provide incentive compensation credit at the time of booking particularly if there is little likelihood of order cancellation, need for customer follow-up, or extensive installation support.

- *Invoice/ship:* Most companies ship products and issue an invoice at the same time. At this point, the accounting system recognizes the order as an account receivable. Use invoice/ship for crediting sales if there is a high rate (over 5 percent) of orders being changed or cancelled between booking and invoice/ship.

- *Installation/customer acceptance:* The next step in the purchase process is the installation/customer acceptance event. Major purchases often require a sign-off by the customer before they will pay the invoice. If sales management wants the salesperson involved in customer acceptance, then credit the sale at the point of installation/customer acceptance for sales compensation purposes.

- *Customer payment:* The final step in the purchase process is the receipt of the customer payment. Most companies recognize sales credit prior to this point, but for sales environments where customer payment is problematic, waiting until the company is paid before granting sales credit would be prudent.

- *Hybrid:* Some companies split the credit with 50 percent credit at booking and 50 percent credit at installation, as an example.

Sales credit timing should reflect the preferred involvement of the salesperson. As a rule: "Credit sales personnel when you no longer want them involved in the sales process."

Sales Credit Adjustments

Most sales compensation plans provide for payment on *net* sales, that is, less returns and sales credits. Sales personnel should not be paid for sales that are not fully realized by the company. Thus net-out (reduce) sales credit by any returns before calculating the incentive payment.

Additionally, some sales organizations also net-out past due receivables that extend beyond a fixed number of days outstanding such as 90 or 120 days. Once past this cut-off time, some companies deny sales credit even if the company eventually collects the money.

Paying on Sales-Out Performance

Indirect sales personnel with end-user business development respon-sibilities have a unique challenge to document sales credit for what they influenced. For example, sales personnel who sell personal com-puters and software through distributors and value-added resellers do not write end-user orders. Normally, they work with the distributor to help promote products through the distributor sales team. Addition-ally, part of their market development responsibilities includes mak-ing end-user sales calls. However, they do not write orders; instead, they refer the opportunity to the channel partners. The channel part-ners take and fulfill the order. Sales management of the manufacturer wants to reward their channel sales representative for driving end-user sales. However, the company does not have the information from the distributors to credit sales—which products were sold to which customers. This type of information is known as *sales-out* data. Of course, the channel partner has this data; but they are not inclined to share it with the manufacturing company. Why? They do not want the manufacturer to "take the line direct" and thus lose valuable cus-tomers. However, many manufacturers negotiate a financial arrange-ment with their channel partners to provide the sales-out data for either a fee or discount on the purchase of products.

Sales Credit Audits

Sales management should expect unexpected and sometimes unusual and out-of-policy sales crediting requests from the field sales forces. Mandate that no out-of-policy sales crediting can occur without sen-ior sales management approval. Make the finance department your partner and schedule annual audits of sales crediting practices.

"Rolling Death"—a union negotiates a new crediting practice. The general manager of a telephone directory company was puzzled to learn that the business agent for the unionized sales force—a rar-ity in itself—wanted to lower sales personnel pay. *The last contract negotiated between the company and union changed when sales credit would occur from payment receipt to the time of booking—a positive feature sought by the union. To protect the company, the new* *contract also added a companion feature requiring full commission payback if customers cancelled or reduced orders. Because of a high level of negative adjustments between booked value and actual payment, some sales personnel began to carry substantial payout obligations to the company. Known as "rolling death" because it carried over from one performance period to the next, many sales personnel wanted this provision removed from the contract and were willing to accept a pay reduction to accomplish this. Preferred Solution: Because of the high number of adjustments between order and payment, the right solution is to go back to the previous practice of providing sales credit at the time of payment and not at the time of booking.*

Summary

Sales compensation works in conjunction with important sales management programs of territory configuration, quota management, and sales crediting. When undertaking a sales compensation redesign effort, sales management must examine these programs also. Large and complex sales organizations must be mindful not to allow these programs to contradict or negate the focus of the sales compensation plan. Policies and procedures governing these support programs need mindful attention. When properly aligned, all contribute to an effective sales performance management program.

8

Administration

Sales compensation requires attentive administration and, in some cases, powerful automation tools. When done well, effective administration acts as an unseen but indispensable program foundation. To be successful, the sales compensation program needs responsive headquarters administration and unerring execution. Support for the sales compensation plan by sales personnel is a combination of aspiration, compliance, and trust. Ineffective administration can quickly erode participant trust. Inaccurate checks, incorrect crediting, late payments, and confused reporting will expend a sales force's goodwill. As the performance periods unfold from weeks to months, from months to quarters, and from quarters to annual measurement periods, sales personnel depend on the administration system to provide an accurate statement of their performance, and thus, pay. Often considered a back-office function, underresourced administration can cause significant dissatisfaction in sales personnel and, even worse, create field flare-ups where frustration is so high that sellers stop selling as they await resolution of their confused incentive payments.

In this chapter, we will examine the components and best practices of effective sales compensation administration.

Administration Components

Administration is a combination of policies, procedures and accountabilities, automation, and reporting. While the exact configuration of these functions differs from one company to another, they are inescapable components of sales compensation administration. Effective sales compensation requires proper provisioning of the administrative function.

Once a design team has rendered its preferred design and the plan has been approved by senior management, it then moves into the domain of program administration. Program administration covers all day-to-day operation of the sales compensation program. The following components comprise sales compensation administration:

- *Policies:* Policies specify the rules associated with the treatment of credits, quotas, employment status, and formula calculations.
- *Procedures and accountabilities:* Procedures provide the action steps for program execution. Accountabilities delineate individuals responsible for various administrative functions.
- *Automation:* The scope of automation support depends on the complexity and intensity of sales compensation transactions.
- *Reporting:* Sales compensation reporting includes providing meaningful information to diverse audiences such as sales personnel, sales management, headquarters management, and administrators.

The following sections provide a brief overview of each of these administrative components as well as suggestions for good practices and what to avoid.

Policies

Sales compensation policies are just the opposite of what you would expect from a sales compensation program: They are dry and not very inspirational. Sales management must provide detailed policy statements. Use the following checklist to ensure that you have the necessary documented policy statements:

- *Account assignments:* How are account assignment changes made—under what conditions? What sales credit rights do sales personnel have after accounts move in or out of territories? When are accounts moved for temporary purposes? How should temporary assignment of accounts affect sales credit and quotas? What happens when external account factors affect account status such as when companies are moved, acquired, or shuttered? Who approves account changes?
- *Quota management:* How is quota allocation done? How can quotas be changed? What is the petition process for quota adjustments? How will quota changes affect incentive compensation? Who approves quota allocation assignments and quota assignment changes?

- *Sales crediting:* What is the definition of a sales credit for sales compensation purposes? Who gets direct credit for a sale? How is sales credit split? When can double sales credit be awarded? What happens if orders are changed or cancelled? How is customer late payment treated? How is customer nonpayment treated? What accounting system report provides the official point of recognition for sales credit? How are sales credit petition adjustments submitted? Who has final approval on sales credit changes and adjustments?

- *Program timing:* When are territories assigned? When is quota allocation done? When are program changes announced? When do they take effect? When are exceptions and adjustments considered? When is the cutoff date and/or time for performance period crediting? When will checks be issued? When will approved adjustments be reflected in the incentive payment?

- *Program interpretations, exceptions, and adjustments:* Who is responsible for program interpretations? What exceptions will be considered? Which types of exceptions will not be considered? What form do adjustments take?

- *Benefit program treatment:* Which, if any, benefit programs for sales personnel differ from other company employees? How are the following calculated: vacation pay, holiday pay, life insurance values, retirement contributions, 401K contributions and company matching portions, flexible benefit deductions, and stock purchase programs?

- *Sales expenses:* Which sales expenses are reimbursed? How do sales personnel submit expenses? When are expenses reimbursed? What documentation is needed? How is use of personal automobiles treated? What financial obligation does the salesperson carry for use of a company car? What does the company provide, for example, mobile phone, wireless e-mail, personal digital assistant (PDA), pager, laptop, high-speed access away from the office?

- *Employment status:* How is the sales compensation program affected by new hire status, promotions, temporary assignments, transfers, terminations, sickness, death, and retirement? How is pay affected by time devoted to local sales meetings, training programs, and national sales conferences?

- *Governance:* Who has final program authority for the sales compensation program? Who needs to approve changes, amendments, and exceptions to the program?

- *Rights and obligations:* What rights and obligations do sales personnel have under the sales compensation program? What are management's rights and obligations under the sales compensation program?

- *Personal integrity:* What personal integrity expectations does management hold for sales personnel? What are the consequences for not upholding these expectations?

While sometimes off-handedly referred to as boilerplate, do not be fooled into thinking that these policies are unimportant or that they exist as an understanding. Every sales compensation plan document should contain a policy statement section covering *all* of the above topics.

"We are a small company with three sales reps. Do we need all this policy stuff?" Well, yes. Size and management style cannot abrogate your responsibilities to prepare clear and unambiguous policy statements regarding the pay plan. Without such clarity, you run the risk of unpleasant legal action at worst, and distracted, wary salespeople at best.

Procedures and Accountabilities

Procedures provide a step-by-step description of how to execute the sales compensation program. Numerous responsible parties contribute to making the sales compensation program a success. Prepare a workflow chart to communicate accountabilities and timing. Each of the following subjects should have its own workflow chart:

- Account assignment
- Quota management
- Sales crediting
- Data assembly and audit
- Incentive calculation
- Reporting
- Audit and assessment
- Exceptions and adjustments

The best documentation of procedures makes it possible for any individual to take over a task and quickly assume the duties with little disruption in execution. In other words, procedures and accountabilities describe who should do what when. Figure 8-1 is an illustration of a workflow chart for quota allocation. This only represents a stylized example. Complete workflow charts provide more detail.

Detailed workflow diagrams provide a road map of procedure steps and accountabilities. Once approved, render these charts into action steps. Publish these procedure action steps for each administrative function.

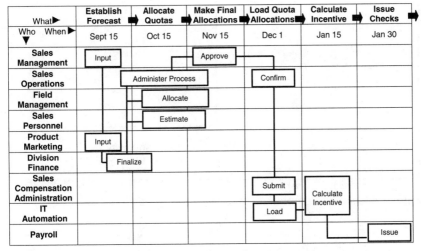

Figure 8-1. Quota Allocation Workflow Chart

Automation

Today's compensation administrator can choose from among many automation alternatives including: desktop applications, custom solutions, dedicated applications, and program suite options. The selection of the right automation choice depends on information processing needs and costs. Of course, as processing needs arise, so do costs—both direct (purchase price) and indirect (staff and field time) devoted to data input, processing, maintenance, and reporting. Automation needs are calibrated on two variables:

- *Complexity:* Jobs, measures, crediting rules, and mid-year program changes drive complexity.

- *Intensity:* Intensity reflects the number of incumbents, transactions, and duration of measurement periods.

Figure 8-2 illustrates the relationship among these variables.

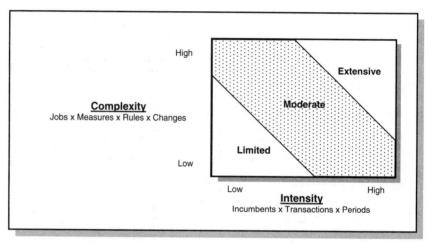

Figure 8-2. Sales Compensation Automation Needs

Figure 8-3 illustrates how automation requirements differ by need. Sales compensation administrators can select from among the following automation choices:

- *Desktop applications:* Use desktop applications such as spreadsheets and simple databases when information processing needs are limited. An assigned administrator keeps the desktop application up-to-date and loads the few transactions per performance period. Be careful not to incorrectly extend the use of desktop applications as complexity and intensity increase.

- *Custom solutions:* Whether developed internally or by an external vendor, custom solutions—those crafted to serve current informa-

	Limited	Moderate	Extensive
Conditions	Fewer than 50 Payees Few Jobs Fewer than 3 Measures Simple Crediting Rules Few Changes Few Transactions Quarterly Periods One Currency	◄────────►	More than 250 Payees Over 15 Jobs 10 Measures or More Complex Crediting Rules Frequent Changes Over 100k/Period Weekly/Monthly Periods Multicurrency
Functionality	*Manual Execution* Payout Calculation Manual Control Payroll File Limited Reporting	◄────────►	*Hands-Free Execution* Input Audit/Cleansing Linked Input Loading Automatic Processing Automatic Status Updates Multi-Reporting Modeling Tools
Data Input	Manual Entry Manual File Transfer Single Data Source No Data Cleansing	◄────────►	Automatic Feeds Numerous Sources Data Reconciliation Multi-Period Tracking
Transaction Processing	Simple Calculation Limited Number Single Time Event No Past Reconciliation No Credit Splits	◄────────►	Numerous Calculations Complex Calculations Multi-Time Periods Numerous Reconciliation Multiple Credit Events High Transaction Count
Maintenance	Few Changes Few Adjustments Limited Updates Stable Quotas Stable Work Force Stable Territories	◄────────►	Many Changes Many Adjustments Extensive Plan Updates Changing Quotas Changing Work Force Changing Territories History Files
Data Output	Payroll File Management Reports	◄────────►	Input Audit Report Exception Reporting Management Reports Incumbent Web Reports Assessment Reports Payroll File Trend Reporting
Cost Modeling	None	◄────────►	Plan Change Impact Multi-Variable Scenarios Sensitivity Testing Market Data Calibration Optimization Choices

Figure 8-3. Automation Needs

tion needs—allow users to have their needs exactly met. The advancement of software development tools has reduced the time to develop such solutions while increasing the power and flexibility of the application. However, changes will require software engineering support.

- *Dedicated application:* Numerous vendors now provide dedicated incentive compensation application software. These products are evolving and range from extremely powerful (and sometimes confusing) to very simple (but with limited capability). Two categories exist: standalone solutions that operate as unique applications and bundled solutions that are part of other front-office software suites.

Finally, the sales compensation administrator can choose from several service models:

- *Installed solution:* An installed solution is the most common service model. Using this approach, a company builds or buys a software application and runs the application on the company's own information technology (IT) system.

- *Hosted solution:* A second service model is to have the application hosted by a third-party vendor that provides data access and information processing via Web links or electronic data transfer methods. This approach helps reduce the burden on internal IT resources.

- *Outsource:* The third choice is to purchase outsourcing support where a third-party vendor provides the complete solution—both application and administrative support. Companies who wish to remove administration completely should purchase this type of service.

Reporting

With rapid advances in information systems and Internet communications, a more expansive palette of reporting choices is now available:

- *Administrator reports:* Administrators need ongoing reporting of program operation as regular production cycles occur: input audit reporting, exception tracking, and current status (organizational reporting, credit assignments, territory assignments, and quota assignments).

- *Senior sales management reports:* Sales leadership needs to monitor the effectiveness, cost, and results of the sales compensation program. Key indices of quota performance, payout levels, and product sales provide a "dashboard" of metrics.

- *Field sales management:* All levels of field sales management require immediate on-line access to current sales performance and trend information. Special reporting capabilities provide information for sales analysis purposes. Additionally, first-line supervisors use detailed sales performance information to help coach individual sales representatives.

- *Product management:* Product management examines product sales information by various factors to gain insight on how to best support the field sales organization.

- *Finance:* Finance accesses sales performance and compensation data to evaluate return on sales expense dollars, administrative compliance, and revenue and profit contribution.

- *Human resources:* Human resources gather sales compensation payout information to evaluate external competitiveness and internal equity.

- *Executive management:* Executive management evaluates the overall effectiveness of the program by reviewing summary analytical reports on program performance.

How to Avoid Unnecessary Administrative Burdens

Without proper management, sales compensation programs can sometimes require unwarranted, elaborate, administrative systems and costly software solutions. To reduce unnecessary administrative burdens, consider the following recommendations:

- *Limit changes:* A certain number of changes need to occur during the program year but limit the number, extent, and scope of changes (quotas, territories, sales crediting, and formula calculation).

- *Exclude volatile and uncertain items:* Exclude from the sales compensation program factors that frequently change and treat them separately. Examples include new product launches, uncertain mega orders, and special product campaigns.

- *Tolerate inequities:* In some cases, trying to keep the sales force whole can create excessive tracking and accounting issues.

- *Control exceptions:* Place a limit on what, why, and when exceptions will be considered.

- *Limit credit splits:* Limit the use of credit splits and double crediting. Use only when necessary.

- *Limit "following credits":* Do not have sales credits "follow" sales personnel to new territories or job assignments. Buy out any credit rather than use tracking of actual credits.

Summary

Policies, procedures and accountabilities, automation, and reporting are key components of the overall administrative support for effective sales compensation programs. These administrative systems require substantial investment. While not highly visible to sales personnel when functioning correctly, they become very visible (and distracting) when not operating effectively.

9

Implementation and Communication

All sales compensation plans should have a published effective start date and a termination date. The effective period of the compensation program should match the company's fiscal year. The termination of the sales compensation program on an annual basis gives sales management the opportunity to redirect sales force efforts to better serve changing corporate objectives. The anticipated announcement of the new program, with new performance measures, goals, and payout formula, provides sales management with an eager audience. Sales personnel want to learn how to excel under the new pay program. Sales management should fully optimize this leadership opportunity.

The successful launch of a new sales compensation program requires the combination of exceptional program implementation and inspired communication.

Implementation

While the communication about the new pay plan occurs close to the effective start date, implementation efforts begin much earlier. Depending on the scope of changes and the size of the sales force, implementation activities could begin months prior to the effective date of the new pay program.

Implementation Checklist

The following provides a checklist of implementation actions:

- *Program approval and funding:* Before proceeding with implementation actions, obtain program approval from the senior management team. Depending on internal practices, this process may be informal and cursory or require extensive documentation and final signature concurrence. Senior management needs to approve both program design and all costs including payout and administrative costs. An approval package should contain the following information:

- New fiscal year sales objectives and goals
- Assessment of current program
- Major revisions with comparison of the new plan to the old plan
- A spreadsheet of all plans with target total compensation, mix, leverage, performance measures, weighting of performance measures, payment periods, and key crediting rules

- *Support programs:* All issues regarding quota management including quota allocation, account assignments, and sales crediting need final resolution prior to program implementation.

- *Automation systems:* Test all automation systems: data input, transaction processing, and output reporting. Conduct several mock runs to fully test the automation program. Provide full testing up to and including payroll file production.

- *Procedures:* Have fully documented administrative procedures with workflow charts, steps, and assigned accountabilities.

Conversion and Transition Methods

Conversion and transition methods provide the means to move from an old plan to a new plan. The extent of the changes is a function of the degree of program change in one or more of the following plan elements:

- *Total target cash compensation (TTCC):* The company may need to increase or decrease TTCC. Increases to total target cash compensation amounts are easy to implement, but reductions are not.

- *Pay mix:* The pay mix may need to change due to changes in eligibility, sales role influence, or labor market practices. When reducing the size of the target incentive, management must increase base salary, often at amounts outside normal base pay changes. However, when management wants to increase the incentive component (without changing the total target cash compensation), the base pay portion must be reduced.

- *Performance measures:* Changing performance measures will require a change in selling activities and focus. In some cases, sales representatives can quickly make the necessary changes. Other types of performance changes may take several months as sales personnel become more proficient (and customers more accepting) of new selling messages.

- *Payment periods:* A change in performance period may affect income cash flow payout to sales personnel. A certain adjustment period may be necessary to accommodate a different payout schedule.

Minor changes to the pay program may require no conversion or transition support. However, major changes—those causing significant pay dislocations—between the old plan and the new plan may require one or more of the following techniques:

- *Cold cut:* A cold-cut approach provides no transition support. If a major change benefits sales personnel, such as giving them a higher base salary with no incentive reduction, then an immediate change is welcomed by all. However, if the change presents significantly new challenges to earn compensation, then a cold cut might be a major burden on sales personnel. The company may face the risk of excessive turnover. However, some management teams use this drastic management intervention to separate those who wish to continue with the company from those who seek their futures elsewhere.

- *Guarantees:* When pay dislocations are significant, sales management might consider providing guarantee payments:
  - *Flat amount:* The easiest is to offer a flat guarantee during a defined transition period with no downside or upside opportunity.
  - *Guarantee with upside:* A favorable guarantee type for sales personnel is to provide upside earnings for sales performance that exceeds the guarantee level.
  - *Declining guarantee:* Another guarantee type is to provide a graduated declining guarantee where the amount of the guarantee is reduced each month until it expires.
  - *Two-check method:* Sales organizations that need to introduce an at-risk program often use the two-check guarantee method. With this approach the payroll department splits the current paycheck into two separate checks: the first represents the new base salary

and the second check represents the new, at-risk incentive element. Management informs the participants that the second check will become variable after the guarantee period expires.

- *Grandfathering:* If the new pay program calls for reducing pay levels, another approach is to grandfather highly paid participants without reducing target pay levels for either base salary or incentive pay.

Conversion Methods: Best Practices. When converting to a new sales compensation program, sales management will find many competing objectives including achieving sales objectives, controlling costs, and not demoralizing or upsetting the sales force. However, some principles can help reconcile some of these conflicting issues. First, the role of the sales compensation program is to drive sales efforts to meet company objectives. Sales management should avoid conversion techniques that unnecessarily delay this intent such as long guarantee periods and grandfathering. Second, buy out any commitment such as carryover credits from previous sales that will distract sales personnel from their current assignments. Lastly, don't delay the inevitable. Accept the fact that not all changes will be popular.

Roll-Out Schedule

Prepare a roll-out schedule including steps and accountabilities for implementation of the sales compensation program. Prepare a comprehensive outline of who, what, when, and where for the roll-out of the new sales compensation program. Of course, the larger the sales organization, the more complex the roll-out effort and thus the need for a more extensive and complete roll-out documentation.

Communication

At its heart, sales compensation is a communication device: It tells salespeople what's important and what's not important. Day after day, the sales compensation program reiterates what management seeks. Sales management wants the sales force to understand the plan, support it, and strive to meet its objectives. The purpose of a well-designed communication effort is to increase sales force commitment to the sales compensation program and its strategic objectives.

An effective communication effort is made up of eight components:

- Communication schedule
- Sales leadership message
- Program launch material
- Field management training
- Sales force communication
- Plan documentation
- Performance and payout reporting
- Plan updates and advisory notes

Communication Schedule

Each company will have its own unique time line for its sales compensation communication effort. Start by identifying the most important date—the announcement to the sales force—and work backwards. While effective communication theory recommends making the announcement prior to the plan effective date, most sales executives prefer to announce the new program after the old program has expired so as not to distract sales personnel during the final weeks of the fiscal year. For example, for fiscal years ending December 31st, the new sales compensation program will become effective January 1st. Plan the roll-out of the new sales compensation program to occur *after* January 1st, and as late as the second or third week of January.

Sales Leadership Message

The launch of the new sales compensation program gives the sales executive a superb platform to articulate the sales objectives for the coming year and inspire commitment to sales results. The more personalized the delivery, the more effective the message. Face-to-face communication is better than a live video broadcast; a live video broadcast is better than a DVD/VHS video presentation; a DVD/VHS is better than a nonvideo Web-cast presentation; and a Web-cast presentation is better than a memo.

Figure 9-1 is an example of the tenor of an effective sales leadership message.

A message from the VP of Sales—Your New Sales Compensation Program

I am pleased to announce the new sales compensation program for this coming year! Your manager will be giving you detailed information on how the program works and how it will affect your earning opportunities.

The strength of our company is tied directly to the success of our salespeople. Our customers and our competitors recognize our sales force as a critical competitive element of our success. Without our skilled, motivated, and high-caliber sales personnel, we would not have the success we have today.

However, we cannot live on our past success. We need to be ready and committed to meeting new and demanding sales objectives. These objectives will change from year to year and we must change, too.

A key element to our sales effectiveness is our sales compensation program. Each year we reexamine our pay program to ensure it provides competitive pay opportunities for you and supports our critical sales strategies.

For this coming fiscal year, we need to maintain focus on revenue growth, but with greater attention to profitable revenue growth. In addition to ensuring our pay levels are competitive, we have made adjustments to reward those who achieve profitable sales. If you are a direct seller, you will find a new measure in your pay plan: "price realization." The idea is simple—sell higher volumes and avoid deep discounting to earn exceptional pay.

We are committed to making you successful by providing you with the tools you need to do your job. The new sales compensation plan represents one such solution. We join with you to make this a successful year for the company and for you personally.

Good Selling!

Figure 9-1. Sales Leadership Message

Program Launch Material

Depending on the extent of change and the size of the sales organization, the prepared communication material will vary. Use the following as a checklist for material preparation:

- Sales leadership message
- Field manager communication training material
- Plan documentation
- E-mail announcement
- Web site update

- Employee announcement packet
- Field manager presentation material

Field Management Training

Field managers should present the new sales compensation program to sales personnel. Investment in field manager training provides exponential return on the program effectiveness. Bring region and district managers together for a full-day training program. Devote the first half of the day to plan explanation. For the second half of the day, have the field managers practice their communication presentations.

Sales Force Communication

As with any promotion, multiple communication events from different sources who restate and support the primary theme create focus, understanding, and retention. The following communications events help promote the sales compensation program to the sales personnel:

- *Sales leadership message:* As mentioned before, the sales leadership message provides the foundation for all subsequent sales compensation messages. Ideally this message would be delivered at the national sales meeting, in person, to all sales personnel.

- *Field manager plan introduction:* Region and district managers should introduce the new sales compensation program to their field personnel.

- *Sales supervisor coaching:* In one-on-one sessions, the sales supervisor meets with each sales representative to discuss how the new sales compensation program will affect the salesperson's income. Advice on how to sell effectively to optimize the sales incentive plan will provide the right direction to sales personnel.

- *Web site content:* Most sales organizations now have a sales department portal for all content information related to selling efforts. Devote a section of this sales department portal to sales compensation documentation including plan description, sales leadership messages, Q&A, and policies and procedures. Also, provide a formula calculator to test the payout potential of the program.

- *Questions and answers:* Prepare the expected Q&As that will most likely arise as part of the sales compensation program implementation. See Figure 9-2 for an example.

New Sales Compensation Program
Questions and Answers

Why are we changing the sales compensation plan? The old one was working great.

We need to continue to focus on the Company's business objectives. Our focus is on profitable revenue growth. We want you to share in the results of increasing our profits by negotiating better pricing.

Will my incentive pay be reduced?

We are not reducing the target incentive opportunity. In fact, we are increasing next year's earning potential. However, you must succeed within the definition of the new sales compensation plan. So, you may make more money, or less, depending on how you perform under the new program.

Why is the new plan more complex than the old plan?

While it does, at first glance, seem more complex, it is really simple. The major change is a new measure on profitability.

I have noticed that the threshold has been raised from 70% to now 85%. Why the change?

We are moving to a more performance-based pay plan. In the past, almost every sales person reached the threshold. Now, we want to give the threshold meaning. If you are not achieving at least 85% of your goal, then we need to review how we can help you to succeed.

How does our incentive plan stack up with others in our industry?

Our HR department tracks our competitive pay position very carefully. They participate in industry surveys of pay practices. Our objective is to provide outstanding pay for outstanding performance, average pay for average performance, and low pay for low performance. While each company's formula may differ, our actual pay levels are very consistent with our objectives.

Will timing of payouts be different?

No, you will continue to earn your volume incentive monthly and your strategic objective performance quarterly.

How will I know what my payout will be?

We have a new Web site (www.salesourcompany.com) that allows you to review your performance statement real time. The site also provides an estimate of how much you will earn if your performance continues with its current trend.

Figure 9-2. Questions and Answers

Plan Documentation

Prepare a complete sales compensation plan document for each plan. Include the following sections in the plan document:

1. *Introduction and strategic objective:* The opening section provides an overview of the strategic objectives for the sales job and how the sales compensation program supports these goals.

2. *Compensation philosophy:* A brief statement provides an overview of the company's competitive position and role of incentive compensation.

3. *Plan overview:* The plan overview section provides an overview of the plan components and their intent.

4. *Plan elements:* This section explains each element of the compensation plan, for example, base salary, volume incentive, and strategic bonus.

5. *Program policies:* Describe applicable territory configuration, quota management, and sales crediting policies in this section.

6. *Formula calculation example:* Provide one or more formula calculation examples showing how the pay plan functions.

7. *Employment status policies:* This section outlines how employment status (transfers, promotions, terminations, retirement, and death) affect the incentive plan.

8. *Rights and obligations:* Legal rights and obligations presented in this section include plan governance and exceptions.

9. *Glossary:* Provide a glossary of terms for easy plan interpretation.

(See Appendix A for an example of a sales compensation plan document.) Have sales personnel sign the performance plan summary that describes their territory, quota, and target incentive amount.

For paperless confirmation, have the salesperson click on a box on the Web site to confirm that he or she has read and understands the sales compensation plan. Make no payments until this electronic acceptance is obtained.

Performance and Payout Reporting

To provide the real-time reinforcement of the incentive plan, provide comprehensive and timely reports on sales performance and payouts. Sales personnel should be able to see all transactions, adjustments, credits, and payout amounts with relative ease. Drill-down Web sites are ideal for providing this level of always-ready detail. Add informative motivational features to the reports by displaying the performance and pay information in charts that show progress year-to-date, year-over-year, and individual progress as compared to the salesperson's peer group. Provide other interested parties with program reports on a regular basis.

Plan Updates and Advisory Notes

Provide a means to issue plan updates and advisory notes regarding plan interpretation. Use a memo format for non-Web-based plan communication. Have multiple approval signatures. Designate a central repository for these updates, changes, and advisory notes.

No Change This Year?

What if your company requires no change? The strategy, job content, and performance measures have not changed. What should you do? Don't miss the opportunity to use the annual review of the plan to restate and support the ongoing strategy. A new plan year still provides the same opportunity to reach out and communicate with sales personnel.

Summary

Implementation and communication activate the sales compensation program. Carefully plan the implementation steps. Leave nothing to chance. Confirm accountabilities, test and retest system solutions, and monitor progress.

Think of the communication program not as an administrative event, but as an advertising and/or marketing event. Make use of the creative talents within your company to develop a theme to market the new sales compensation program to the sales force. Make sure all levels of sales management participate in the process. Use personal communication whenever possible. Your actions will tell the sales force how to act—if you think it's important, they will think it's important. If you don't think it's important—and you suboptimize your communication opportunity—your salespeople won't think it's important either.

10

Program Assessment

How effective is the sales compensation program? It's a simple question and is often asked by senior management. The company expends significant amounts of money on the sales force, especially on the compensation paid to sales personnel.

But is it working? Is the company getting the right sales force focus? Is the sales force motivated by the pay program?

Use the following five factors to assess the sales compensation program:

- *Strategic alignment:* How well does the plan support the company's business objectives?

- *Employee motivation:* Do the sales personnel strive to earn incentive pay by excelling on the program performance measures?

- *Best practice variance:* While some companies will intentionally vary from best practices, knowing these variances may help identify unexpected consequences.

- *Return on investment:* Is the company getting an effective return on investment?

- *Program management:* Is the program management consistent with plan documentation? Is it timely? Accurate?

Each year, sales management should undertake a full, formal review on all five of these factors. For sales organizations facing volatile market conditions, more frequent assessments may be necessary.

Strategic Alignment

The sales compensation program needs to support the company's business objectives. An assessment of the sales compensation program begins with a review of how well the compensation program supports the strategic objectives of the company.

Begin with a confirmation of the company's objectives. Gather any written statements of financial, product, and customer goals, and then proceed with senior management interviews. These interviews will provide contemporary confirmation of the goals of the company. Include both the vice president level and other headquarters personnel interviews including finance, product management, marketing, and sales leadership. Prepare a summary statement of sales objectives for review and confirmation by senior management.

Next, review all the performance measures in the sales compensation program to assess how each measure contributes to achieving the company's objectives. Examine the importance of each measure by reviewing the relative weighting of the measures.

Finally, examine the performance payout information by performance measure to see the relationship between compensation and performance.

Figure 10-1 displays the relationship between total pay and sales volume. The relationship is moderate. This would suggest further investigation to examine how incentive pay relates to quota performance.

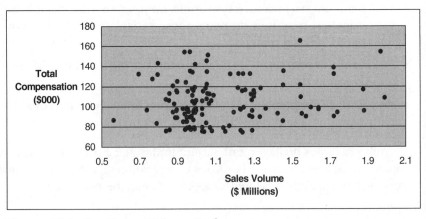

Figure 10-1. Pay Versus Volume Performance

As we can see in Figure 10-2, when compared to quota performance, incentive pay is more closely correlated, which means that the pay system provides greater incentive rewards as sales volume quota performance improves.

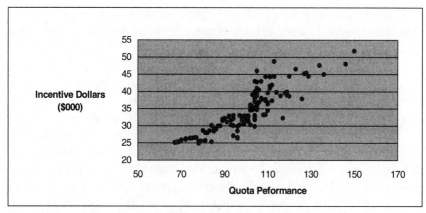

Figure 10-2. Incentive Pay Versus Quota Performance

A similar analysis can be done with gross margin performance. In Figure 10-3, total compensation is compared to gross margin performance.

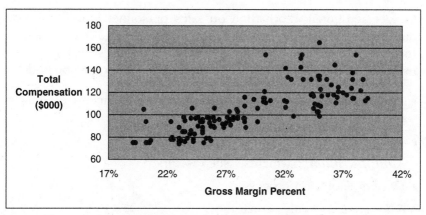

Figure 10-3. Pay Versus Profit

Examine the relationship between pay and performance using a variety of dispersion charts to review trends and pay and performance relationships. Prepare unique charts for each job. Be careful to eliminate data of personnel who only worked part of the year.

Using the dispersion charts, determine what the program really rewards versus what it purports to reward.

Going out of business, slowly. Unbeknown to management, the incentive plan of a large regional chain of coffee/doughnut shops was putting the company out of business. *In an effort to improve profits, the new financially centric management team introduced an incentive plan to reduce baking waste. Because each store baked its own fresh product, the new incentive plan was designed to discourage excess production. Store managers in an attempt to lower the waste rate produced fewer doughnuts than were needed. This had a subtle yet negative impact on customer service. As the years passed, the cycle of low production led to declining customer traffic, which led to further reduction in production, which led to further reduction in customer traffic, and so on. Preferred Solution: Revamp the whole market concept. Introduce new products, push sales with a new marketing campaign, and provide a new pay system to reward revenue growth.*

Employee Motivation

Collect additional information on sales personnel motivation. Conduct field interviews and focus group interviews to learn what features of the incentive program are effective. Gather survey responses using Web-based surveys. Ask questions about the following items:

- *Plan effectiveness:* total compensation, target incentive pay, program focus
- *Communication:* understanding of the plan
- *Administration:* payments, issue resolution
- *Quotas:* allocation process, fairness
- *Sales crediting:* rules, consistency
- *Recognition plan:* impact
- *Contests:* effectiveness

Sales management should also ask sales personnel this very simple question: Does the sales compensation program motivate you to achieve the company's objectives?

Finally, examine both new hire acceptances and voluntary termination rates. Determine why applicants decline offers. Use a telephone follow-up or a questionnaire. Be specific; ask if the pay program is competitive. Analyze turnover rates to ensure that high-performing personnel are staying and low-performing personnel are departing.

Best Practice Variance

Well-designed sales compensation programs share similar design characteristics. Use this list to review each sales compensation plan:

- *Eligibility:* Eligibility for sales compensation should be reserved for those jobs where the incumbents (1) have customer contact, (2) persuade the customer to act, and (3) contribute to the revenue production of the company.

- *Mix:* Pay mix, the split of total target cash compensation (TTCC) between target base salary and target incentive, should reflect the degree of influence of the job. Where sales personnel have high influence over the customer's decision to buy, provide a low base salary and a high incentive opportunity. Where sales personnel represent only one factor affecting the buyer's decision, provide a high base salary component while keeping the target incentive component smaller.

- *Leverage:* As confirmed by market data, ensure that the best performers—the 90th percentile of job incumbents—earn 3 times the target incentive amount for outstanding performance. Avoid caps on the sales compensation plan.

- *Performance measures and weights:* Always have a revenue production measure to drive sales volume performance. Restrict the number of measures to 3 or fewer. Weight the measures to reflect importance of the measures.

- *Quotas distribution:* The target is for two-thirds of sales personnel to reach and exceed quota and one-third not to reach quota. There should be no bias in the quota allocation process. As Figure 10-4 illustrates, the size of territories should not have a positive or negative influence on the quota performance.

- *Performance and payment periods:* Match the payment period to the performance period. Use cumulative-to-date payments when payouts occur more frequently than the performance period.

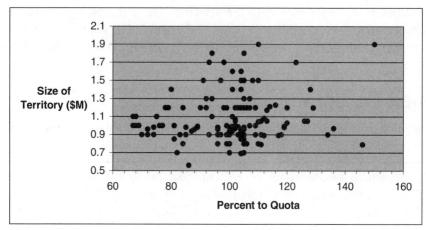

Figure 10-4. Quota Fairness

- *Formula type:* Use a target incentive commission formula when territories are equal; use a target incentive bonus formula when revenue levels among territories are significantly dissimilar.

- *Market data:* Set pay levels consistent with market pay data. Participate in market surveys conducted by a third party featuring uniform data submission standards, mandatory job matching sessions, and incumbent-based data collection and reporting. Purchase surveys annually. Ensure to have more than one survey source for each benchmark job.

Return on Investment

Sales management can monitor the cost of the sales force, specifically the sales compensation program (see Figure 10-5). Regular trend analysis provides a means to track return on sales expense.

Program Management

Evaluation of program management includes the following:

- *Conformity to plan design:* How well does the application of the incentive plan match the plan documentation?

- *Accuracy of payments:* How accurate are payout calculations? What is the error and/or correction rate?

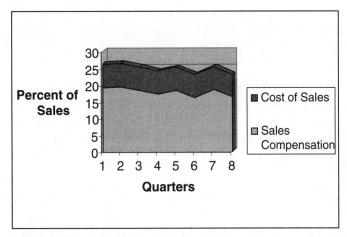

Figure 10-5. Sales Costs

- *Timeliness of payments:* Are payout checks issued at the stated time?

- *Resolution of exceptions:* How quickly do exceptions take to resolve?

- *Scope of reporting:* How extensive is the reporting of the sales compensation program to meet the needs of headquarters management, field sales management, and individual sales representatives?

- *Cost of administration:* How costly is it to administer the sales compensation program?

- *Annual audit:* How did the sales compensation program fare under the annual audit of the program conducted by the finance department?

Common Sales Compensation Symptoms
Here are several examples of common sales compensation symptoms:

1. Unmotivated and frustrated sales personnel: Something is wrong when sales personnel are unmotivated and frustrated. Careful examination of the incentive plan will determine if poor design features of the sales compensation program are contributing to this negative situation.

2. Unpredictable over- or underpayments: The pay plan should not hold "surprises" for either the sales personnel or sales management. Unexpected drops in income or excessive earnings means the sales compensation plan most likely has design errors.

3. Excessive double crediting: The sales compensation program should not rely on excessive double- or split-crediting to function correctly. Examine job design and sales crediting practices when horizontal sales credit exceeds real sales revenue by more than 115 percent.

Summary

An assessment of the sales compensation program requires a multifactor review: strategic alignment, employee motivation, best-practice variance, return on investment, and program management. Some companies use a standing sales compensation review committee to monitor program effectiveness. Other companies make it a periodic project. Regardless, a comprehensive review of the sales compensation program should occur on an annual basis.

11

Sales Compensation Design

Sales management should plan well in advance for a full redesign of the sales compensation program. Sales compensation redesign is an iterative process. For large sales organizations, this process could take up to 4 to 5 months elapse time. Smaller sales organizations, with 10 to 50 sales representatives with 3 or fewer sales jobs should start their redesign efforts at least 2 months in advance of the implementation date. Sales organizations with fewer than 10 sales personnel should give themselves at least a month elapse time for sales compensation design efforts.

Why is "tweaking" bad? Making minor adjustments to the sales compensation program on an annual basis is an acceptable and preferred practice when underlying influencing factors have changed very little. However, be wary of the practice of tweaking the sales compensation program. What is the difference between minor adjustments and tweaking? Minor adjustments assume that sales management has made a complete review of all the plans and the limited changes fit within the context of the overall program design. Tweaking, however, makes isolated changes and patches to the pay program outside the context of the overall design. While such changes often reflect good intentions, the summation of these tweaks can create confusing and convoluted sales compensation plans.

The Sales Compensation Design Process

An important element of the sales compensation design process is the involvement and participation of key stakeholders. As the design steps presented below suggest, various points within the design process require collaborative decision-making. These involvement steps are needed to help resolve competing objectives and make tough resource allocation decisions. For example, when selecting performance measures, the senior management team needs concurrence on the use of the right measures to ensure alignment with the company's objectives. Unfortunately, sales, finance, operations, and marketing may have different and competing expectations for the sales force. Leaders of these departments need to meet to identify key measures for inclusion in (or exclusion from) the sales compensation program. Likewise, similar collaborative decision-making is necessary when providing automation provisioning for the sales compensation program. Sales operations, finance, and information technology (IT) need to review various choices affecting functionality and costs.

This collaborative approach is a vote against the expert-recommended solution. Whether concocted by an inside resource, the vice president of sales, or an outside consultant, such expert solutions are often counterproductive. There is no right answer to sales compensation design. The right answer is a shared judgment by the leadership team. The leadership team needs to "work the issue" to examine implications and impacts of various alternatives as they attempt to drive company objectives.

Ten Steps to Sales Compensation Design

Regardless of the size of the organization and the elapse time devoted to the redesign effort, the following 10 steps provide a road map for all sales organizations. Each step provides a crucial element to ensure successful redesign. This process should be repeated every year.

Step 1: Fact Finding

The first step is to gather information about the current program and confirm the company's business objectives. Undertake the following actions to prepare a *Fact Finding Report*:

- *Interview senior management:* Gather perspectives regarding the current program and information about future sales objectives from senior management.

- *Interview headquarters staff:* Learn what is working with the current pay program and where improvements are needed. Gather all written documentation regarding the current and proposed jobs and organization structure. Collect all information about the current pay programs including policies and practices related to account assignment, quota allocation, and sales crediting.

- *Interview field sales management:* Collect field perspectives regarding the effectiveness of the current program. Capture any suggestions for changes.

- *Interview sales personnel:* Learn how sales personnel view the current sales compensation program. Assess their understanding of the current plan. Gain their views on how to improve the program. Document job content. Ask sales personnel to confirm how the current sales compensation program supports the charter of their sales job. For large sales forces, gather electronic survey responses on the effectiveness of the sales compensation program.

- *Purchase external survey data:* Obtain competitive market data from compensation survey sources. (See Appendix B for a partial listing.)

- *Assemble pay and performance data:* Gather quantitative information on the current program—pay and performance data.

- *Obtain strategic goals:* Solicit internal documentation on the forthcoming strategic goals of the company.

- *Document mid-year changes:* Gather all mid-year changes including program design, account assignment changes, quota changes, and sales personnel movement.

Step 2: Assessment

Conduct analytical and comparative assessment analysis. Conduct the following analysis for inclusion in the Assessment Report.

- *Make competitive market comparison:* Compare actual pay levels with labor market practices.

- *Examine pay and performance relationship:* Prepare dispersion charts showing the relationship between performance and incentive payouts.

- *Test quota system:* Examine the quota system for proper balance of performance below and above quota. Ensure the program is free of unintended bias.

- *Review performance measures:* Determine if performance measures support the company's business objectives.

- *Calculate return on investment:* Prepare trend charts showing the change in cost of sales and return on investment.

- *Audit support programs:* Review support programs to ensure compliance with policies for account assignment, quota allocation, and sales crediting.

Step 3: Alignment

The alignment step provides senior management with its first collaborative involvement in the design process. During this step of the project, senior management reviews a summary of the *Fact Finding Report* and *Assessment Report* prepared for Steps 1 and 2, respectively. Then working as a group, the senior team including the general manager, top sales executive, top finance executive, top marketing executive, and head of human resources will confirm the *Sales Alignment Statement* that includes:

- *Corporate sales strategy:* Specify the strategic role of the sales force regarding revenue, profit, product, and customer strategies.

- *Sales compensation principles:* Examine sales compensation design principles regarding eligibility, total target cash compensation (TTCC), mix, leverage, performance measures, quota allocation, and pay and performance periods for appropriateness. Update the sales compensation principles as appropriate.

Step 4: Program Design

For Step 4, assemble a design task force consisting of sales management, marketing, finance, and human resources to examine design alternatives and select a preferred design. For small organizations, the design task force will most likely be those who authored the *Sales Alignment Statement.* Larger sales organizations might appoint specialists from each department to serve on the task force. Companies that have multiple sales entities should assemble a design task force for each sales unit. The task force develops preferred sales compensation designs during the following meetings:

- *Meeting 1: Review of current documentation:* Present and discuss all relevant material: *Fact Finding Report, Assessment Report* and *Sales Alignment Statement.* If participants are new to the design of sales compensation, provide an overview of key sales compensation concepts.

- *Meetings 2 and 3: Design sales compensation plans:* Work through the sales compensation design for each job. Design by element, not by job. Use Figure 11-1, an example of a spreadsheet, to record design decisions.

Job Title	Eligible	TTCC	Mix	Leverage	Measures	Weighting	Formula Type
Worldwide Sales Executive	Yes	$250K	80/20	3x	Volume	75%	Bonus
					Profit	25%	Bonus
Sr. Sales Representative	Yes	$150K	75/25	3x	Volume	50%	Bonus
					Retention	50%	Bonus
Territory Representative	Yes	$75K	60/40	3x	Volume	75%	Commission
					New Accounts	25%	Bonus
Telephone Sales	Yes	$65K					
Product Overlay	Yes						

Figure 11-1. Sales Compensation Design Elements

- *Meeting 4: Confirm preferred designs:* Review proposed sales compensation designs. Make necessary adjustments.

Step 5: Support Programs

A team of sales management personnel prepares guidelines for the territory configuration, quota management, account assignment, and sales crediting rules. Develop estimates of territory loading, quota allocation numbers, and the impact of various sales crediting practices. Prepare a *Support Program Impact Report.*

Step 6: Modeling and Costing

The sales operations function examines cost by modeling the overall program costs and preparing individual income estimates. Provide these to senior management for approval in a *Program Cost Report.*

Step 7: Automation

Assemble a work team of specialists from sales operations, finance, and information technology (IT) to examine automation alternatives and select a preferred system. Get approval and funding for a solution. (See Appendix C for a list of incentive software vendors.) Test automation solution prior to program launch.

Step 8: Implementation

Prepare an implementation schedule for program roll-out, conversion, communication, and systems support. Allocate responsibilities to assigned personnel for each component of the implementation effort.

Step 9: Communication

Prepare communication collateral, train field managers, and populate Web site with relevant content.

Step 10: Administration

Prepare administrative procedures and practices. Communicate accountabilities and time commitments to responsible personnel.

Ten Steps—Work Plan

Prepare a work plan (see Figure 11-2) to track progress of the sales compensation redesign effort.

Summary

The sales compensation design process requires a dedicated effort. Appoint a process leader to facilitate the design process. Ensure you have adequate time to accomplish each of the design steps. Conduct the process each year. Follow these 10 steps to keep the compensation plans contemporary with current sales strategies.

Project Steps	1	2	3	4	5	6	7	8	9	10	11	12	13	14	15	16	17
1. Fact Finding	▓	▓															
2. Assessment		▓	▓														
3. Alignment			▓	▓													
4. Program Design					▓	▓											
5. Support Programs					▓	▓	▓	▓	▓								
6. Modeling and Costing									▓	▓	▓						
7. Automation									▓	▓	▓	▓	▓	▓			
8. Implementation												▓	▓	▓	▓	▓	▓
9. Communication														▓	▓	▓	
10. Administration																▓	▓

Figure 11-2. Sales Compensation Work Plan—Weeks

Closing Notes

Sales compensation provides sales management with a powerful tool to help focus sales personnel efforts. However, as we have learned, building an effective sales compensation plan is not a casual task. Following the approach and concepts presented in this book, you will find the task accomplishable. Here are some summary notes as you undertake your sales compensation design efforts.

- *Sales compensation works.* While not appropriate for all selling jobs, sales compensation provides the means to reward superior sales results. Sales personnel respond to the opportunity to perform well.

- *Sales compensation is one of many types of incentive compensation plans.* Sales compensation plans feature a substantial upside opportunity for placing part of the target compensation at risk. Other pay plans such as gainsharing, add-on, and management bonus plans serve different and worthy purposes.

- *Income producers and sales representatives are paid differently.* Income producers earn a portion of their sales production. Sales representatives earn a percent of target incentive, less than for below-expected performance, more for above-expected performance.

- *Sales compensation follows job design.* Sales compensation plans support sales job design. Changes in strategy and focus will change the sales jobs. If the sales job changes, so must the sales compensation plan.

- *Sales compensation administration requires resources.* Whether as head count or automation support, the sales compensation program requires company resources for ongoing success.

- *Collaborative design process promotes the best solution.* Involving key decision makers in the design process will significantly improve the outcome of the design process.

- *Communicate, communicate, and communicate.* Use every means to communicate the new plan to participants.

With the right investment of time in the right design process, you can capitalize on the driven enthusiasm of sales personnel earning outstanding pay for exceeding company objectives!

Appendix A
Illustrative Sales Compensation Plan

Utility Energy, Inc.
Sales Compensation Plan
Sales Representatives
For Plan Year
20xx

Utility Energy, Inc.
20xx Compensation Plan—Sales Representatives

Table of Contents

Introduction

This document presents the Sales Compensation Plan (for Sales Representatives) for Utility Energy, Inc.

Your compensation plan rewards incremental increases in sales performance with incremental increases in compensation earnings. As you improve your sales performance, you will have the opportunity to achieve outstanding earnings.

Section 1: Plan Overview

Why do we need a compensation plan?

The immediate success of Utility Energy, Inc., depends on our ability to rapidly penetrate mid-level business customers outside our traditional service area. To meet these objectives, our compensation plan will provide the following:

- Unique compensation solutions that match plan designs with job responsibilities and desired behaviors
- Focused plan elements that drive achievement of business objectives and selling strategy
- Significant rewards for high achievers

Compensation Philosophy

In general, this plan is intended to communicate a compensation philosophy consistent with the following points:

- **Strategic.** The plan designs will support, drive, and encourage vision and overall business strategy achievement of Utility Energy, Inc. Our goal is to target mid-level customers.
- **Competitive.** The Sales Compensation Plan is designed to attract and retain top performers. We will reward outstanding performance with exceptional earnings opportunities.
- **Fair.** We will develop compensation policies that reward individual achievement in support of sales goals.
- **Simple.** We have designed the new plan to ensure that the mechanics and policies are easy to understand and communicate.

Competitive Earnings

We are committed to the success of Utility Energy, Inc. We provide competitive earnings to those of you who can help us attain our goals. Those who consistently sell at the highest levels of volume will earn the highest levels of compensation.

Section 2: 20xx Sales Compensation Plan Components

The 20xx Compensation Plan consists of two components: Base Salary and MWH (megawatts per hour) units commission based on achievement of unit sales and number of contracts completed.

Base Salary

All individuals covered under the new compensation plan will receive a base salary. The base salary is managed within a pay range. Merit increases are provided on an annual basis consistent with the company's salary merit increase guidelines.

MWH Units and Number of Contracts Commission

The MWH Units and Number of Contracts Commission are based on the number of megawatt hours sold and number of contracts completed at the individual level. Payout will begin once MWH unit sales are equal to or exceed 80,000 and the number of contracts is equal to or exceeds 10. For example, performance of 80% of target (96,000 MWHs and 24 contracts) will yield 50% of target payout ($17,280). Performance at target (120,000 MWHs and 30 contracts) will yield 100% of the target payout ($34,800). Performance above the target level will receive an accelerated commission payout. For example, performance of 120% of target (144,000 MWHs and 36 contracts) will yield 130% of the target payout ($44,640).

Commission Rate per MWH

Contracts	MWH 80,000–120,000	> 120,000
10–19	.08	.09
20–29	.18	.20
30–39	.29	.31
40–49	.31	.37
50+	.33	.44

Note a minimum incentive of $21,875 will be guaranteed for the first year of the plan (20xx). This represents 100% of quarter 1, 75% of quarter 2, 50% of quarter 3, and 25% of quarter 4 target earnings. (See table below.)

Guaranteed Incentive Table

Quarter	Percent Target Earnings Guaranteed	Payout Amount Guaranteed	Cumulative Payout Guaranteed
1	100%	$8,750.00	$ 8,750.00
2	75%	$6,562.50	$15,312.50
3	50%	$4,375.00	$19,687.50
4	25%	$2,187.00	$21,875.00

Section 3: 20xx Sales Compensation Plan Policies and Definitions

Purpose

The purpose of the Utility Energy, Inc., Compensation Program (the "Program") is to reward Participants for identifying and growing business with new customers.

Definitions

The following terms shall have the following meanings for the purposes of the Program:

- **Award.** The payment of dollars to a Participant as determined by this Program.
- **Company.** Utility Energy, Inc.
- **Disability.** Total disability as defined in the Company's long-term disability plan in effect at the time of disability.
- **Participant.** Any employee of the Company who is selected to participate in the Program.
- **Threshold.** In order to receive an incentive payout, it is a requirement for all Participants of this Program to exceed a minimum accomplishment of plan.

- **Incentive Payout.** For all Participants, incentive will accumulate from dollar one, but will not be paid until the thresholds for all measures have been exceeded.

- **Large Orders Rule.** If an order is received that exceeds 12,000 MWII, you will only be credited for 12,000. Exceptions to this rule must have approval by the Sales Director and Managing Director prior to the booking of the order.

- **Program.** Utility Energy, Inc., Compensation Program as originally adopted or, if amended or supplemented, as amended or supplemented.

Award Value Determination

Participants will begin earning incentive once their minimum thresholds have been exceeded.

Incentive Payout will be paid quarterly once thresholds are achieved.

Conventional rounding rules apply: $>.5$ round up, $<.5$ round down.

"Large Orders Rule" will be used to limit credit for orders in excess of order size boundary of 12,000 MWH.

Payments

Eligibility to Participate. Participants must hold a job in one of the participating categories for a minimum of 30 consecutive days in the calendar year in order to be eligible for an incentive payout.

If you should leave Utility Energy, Inc., you will receive an incentive payment equivalent to that which you would have received for the last full quarter you worked.

Normal Case. Payments will be made quarterly, as soon as practical after the close of the quarter, but no later than ninety (90) days after the end of the quarter or year. Cumulative incentive earned to date will be calculated each quarter. The amount paid out each quarter will be the cumulative incentive earned to date less any payouts made in previous quarters.

Death, Disability, Retirement, or Termination (Voluntary/Involuntary). If a Participant dies, becomes disabled, retires, or terminates within the meaning of the Program, he/she shall receive an Award for all bookings through the last full quarter of employment, and shall forfeit the Award for any uncompleted quarter.

Promotions/Transfers to Non-Incentive Eligible Positions. If a Participant is promoted or transferred to a job in the Company that is not eligible for any incentive payment, he/she shall be entitled to a pro-rated payment of Awards for any period completed.

Promotions/Transfers to Incentive Eligible Positions. If a Participant is promoted or transferred to a job in the Company that is eligible for incentive, his/her total incentive payment will be prorated based on the amount of time spent in each position.

Partial Year Participation. The structure of the incentive plan is based upon a Participant's full year participation. We also recognize that people can enter the program at any time during the year. In those situations the following will apply:

- Individual Contributors: If an individual is eligible to become a Participant of the Program for a period of less than 12 months, a plan will be assigned based upon the months of eligibility remaining in the calendar year.

Deviations from these guidelines require written approval from the Sales Director and the Managing Director.

Crediting

Megawatt hours sold will be estimated based upon historical usage plus or minus adjustments according to usual company practices. Contracts will be credited when the contract is signed.

Cancellations and Deductions

Contracts canceled within 90 days of the date performance begins on the contract will result in sales being deducted from the representative's attainment.

Amendment and Termination

The Managing Director may terminate the Program at any time, treating any quarter then in effect as having ended as of the date he/she notifies the participants. The Managing Director may from time-to-time amend or revise the Program.

Effective Date

This Program shall become effective on January 1, 20xx.

Gender Plural and Singular

All pronouns and any variation thereof shall be deemed to refer to the masculine, feminine, or neuter as the identity of the person or persons may require. As the context may require the singular may be read as plural and the plural as singular.

Captions

The captions to the sections and paragraphs of the Program are for convenience only and shall not control or affect the meaning or construction of any of its provisions.

Management Judgment

In all cases, management reserves the right to reduce, modify, or withhold awards based upon individual performance or management modification in the Program. Such action requires the written approval of the Sales Director and Managing Director.

Appendix: 20xx Sales Compensation Plan and Calculation Examples

Example 1:
(Target Payout)

Assume: Annual unit sales of 120,000 MWH and 30 contracts.
Commission Rate: .29 (Look up rate on table.)
Calculation: .29 × 120,000 MWH = $34,840

Example 2:

Assume: Annual unit sales of 96,000 MWH and 15 contracts.
Commission Rate: .08 (Look up rate on table.)
Calculation: .08 × 96,000 MWH = $7,680

Example 3:	Assume: Annual unit sales of 150,000 MWH and 50 contracts. Commission Rate: .44 (Look up rate on table.) Calculation: .44 × 150,000 MWH = $66,000
Example 4: *(Quarterly Payout* *Calculation Notes)*	Note: Payouts begin when both MWH units and number of contracts are over threshold levels. If no commission is earned, a portion of the guaranteed amount will be paid out each quarter when thresholds are not reached. Payout for each quarter is the cumulative incentive earned to-date in the year, less previous payout amounts.
Assumptions:	Assume: • Q1 unit sales of 40,000 MWH, in 10 contracts • Q2 unit sales of 48,000 MWH, in 12 contracts • Q3 unit sales of 32,000 MWH, in 15 contracts • Q4 unit sales of 40,000 MWH, in 10 contracts

Quarter 1 Payout

Step	Directions	Quarter 1 Calculation
Step 1: *Determine* *cumulative sales*	Add sales in all quarters to-date.	Sales in all quarters to-date are quarter 1 sales of 40,000 MWH.
Step 2: *Determine* *cumulative* *contracts*	Add contracts in all quarters to-date.	Contracts in all quarters to-date are quarter 1 contracts of 10.
Step 3: *Determine* *commission* *rate*	Look up cumulative performance on table on p. 197 to obtain commission rate.	Performance not on table because 40,000 is less than 80,000 MWH threshold. Hence, no commission rate applies, and no commission incentive is earned.

Commission Rate per MWH

	Cumulative MWH To-Date	
Cumulative Contracts To-Date	80,000–120,000	> 120,000
10–19	.08	.09
20–29	.18	.20
30–39	.29	.31
40–49	.31	.37
50+	.33	.44

Step 4: Calculate cumulative incentive earned to-date	Multiply commission rate by cumulative number of MWHs.	Not applicable since no commission incentive earned.
Step 5: Calculate guaranteed minimum incentive amount	Look up cumulative payout guaranteed for quarter on guaranteed incentive table. If cumulative guaranteed payout is greater than incentive commission earned, then take as cumulative incentive earned.	Guaranteed minimum for quarter 1 is $8,750.

Guaranteed Incentive Table

Quarter	Percent Target Earnings Guaranteed	Payout Amount Guaranteed	Cumulative Payout Guaranteed
1	100%	$8,750.00	$ 8,750.00
2	75%	$6,562.50	$15,312.50
3	50%	$4,375.00	$19,687.50
4	25%	$2,187.00	$21,875.00

| *Step 6:* *Calculate payout for quarter* | Subtract previous quarter earnings from cumulative incentive earned. | No previous quarters, so earnings are $8,750. |

Quarter 2 Payout

Step	Directions	Quarter 2 Calculation
Step 1: *Determine cumulative sales*	Add sales in all quarters to-date.	Quarter 1 + Quarter 2 MWHs = 40,000 + 48,000 = 88,000 MWHs
Step 2: *Determine cumulative contracts*	Add contracts in all quarters to-date.	Quarter 1 + Quarter 2 Contracts = 10 + 12 = 22 Contracts
Step 3: *Determine commission rate*	Look up cumulative sales and cumulative contracts on table below to obtain commission rate.	88,000 is between 80,000 and 120,000 and 22 is between 20 and 29, hence commission rate is .18.

Commission Rate per MWH

Cumulative Contracts To-Date	Cumulative MWH To-Date	
	80,000–120,000	> 120,000
10–19	.08	.09
20–29	.18	.20
30–39	.29	.31
40–49	.31	.37
50+	.33	.44

| *Step 4:* *Calculate cumulative incentive earned to-date* | Multiply commission rate by cumulative number of MWHs. | Cumulative MWHs = 85,000. 88,000 × .18 = $15,840 |

| *Step 5:* *Calculate guaranteed minimum incentive amount* | Look up cumulative payout guaranteed for quarter on guaranteed incentive table. If cumulative guaranteed payout is greater than incentive commission earned, then take as cumulative incentive earned. | Not applicable, since cumulative incentive, $15,840, is greater than $15,312.50. |

Guaranteed Incentive Table

Quarter	Percent Target Earnings Guaranteed	Payout Amount Guaranteed	Cumulative Payout Guaranteed
1	100%	$8,750.00	$ 8,750.00
2	75%	$6,562.50	$15,312.50
3	50%	$4,375.00	$19,687.50
4	25%	$2,187.00	$21,875.00

| *Step 6:* *Calculate payout for quarter* | Subtract previous quarter earnings from cumulative incentive earned. | Quarter 1 earnings are $8,750. Cumulative earnings are $15,840. $15,840 − $8,750 = $7,090 Quarter 2 payout = $7,090 |

Quarter 3 Payout

Step	Directions	Quarter 3 Calculation
Step 1: *Determine cumulative sales*	Add sales in all quarters to-date.	40,000 + 48,000 + 32,000 = 120,000 MWHs
Step 2: *Determine cumulative contracts*	Add contracts in all quarters to-date.	Quarter 1 + Quarter 2 Contracts = 10 + 12 + 15 = 37 Contracts

Step 3:   Look up cumulative   120,000 is in the range
Determine   sales and cumulative   80,000 to 120,000 and
commission rate   contracts on table   37 is between 30 and
    below to obtain   39, hence commission
    commission rate.   rate is .29.

Commission Rate per MWH

Cumulative Contracts To-Date	Cumulative MWH To-Date	
	80,000–120,000	> 120,000
10–19	.08	.09
20–29	.18	.20
30–39	.29	.31
40–49	.31	.37
50+	.33	.44

Step 4:   Multiply commission   Cumulative MWHs =
Calculate   rate by cumulative   120,000. 120,000 ×
cumulative   number of MWHs.   .29 = \$34,800
incentive
earned to-date

Step 5:   Look up cumulative   Not applicable, since
Calculate   payout guaranteed for   cumulative incentive is
guaranteed   quarter on guaranteed   greater than
minimum   incentive table. If   \$19,687.50.
incentive amount   cumulative guaranteed
    payout is greater than
    incentive commission
    earned, then take as
    cumulative incentive
    earned.

Guaranteed Incentive Table

Quarter	Percent Target Earnings Guaranteed	Payout Amount Guaranteed	Cumulative Payout Guaranteed
1	100%	$8,750.00	$ 8,750.00
2	75%	$6,562.50	$15,312.50
3	50%	$4,375.00	$19,687.50
4	25%	$2,187.00	$21,875.00

Step 6: **Calculate payout for quarter**	Subtract previous quarter earnings from cumulative incentive earned.	Quarter 1 earnings are $8,750. Quarter 2 earnings are $7,090. Cumulative earnings are $34,800. $34,800 − $7,090 − $8,750 = $18,160 Quarter 3 payout = $18,160	

Quarter 4 Payout

Step	Directions	Quarter 4 Calculation
Step 1: **Determine cumulative sales**	Add sales in all quarters to-date.	40,000 + 48,000 + 32,000 + 40,000 = 160,000 MWHs
Step 2: **Determine cumulative contracts**	Add contracts in all quarters to-date.	10 + 12 + 15 + 10 = 47 Contracts
Step 3: **Determine commission rate**	Look up cumulative sales and cumulative contracts on table on p. 202 to obtain commission rate.	160,000 is greater than 120,000 and 47 is between 40 and 49, hence commission rate is .37.

Commission Rate per MWH

Cumulative Contracts To-Date	Cumulative MWH To-Date	
	80,000–120,000	> 120,000
10–19	.08	.09
20–29	.18	.20
30–39	.29	.31
40–49	.31	.37
50+	.33	.44

Step 4: *Calculate cumulative incentive earned to-date*	Multiply commission rate by cumulative number of MWHs.	Cumulative MWHs = 160,000. 160,000 × .37 = $59,200
Step 5: *Calculate guaranteed minimum incentive amount*	Look up cumulative payout guaranteed for quarter on guaranteed incentive table. If cumulative guaranteed payout is greater than incentive commission earned, then take as cumulative incentive earned.	Not applicable, since cumulative incentive of $59,200 is greater than $21,875.00.

Guaranteed Incentive Table

Quarter	Percent Target Earnings Guaranteed	Payout Amount Guaranteed	Cumulative Payout Guaranteed
1	100%	$8,750.00	$ 8,750.00
2	75%	$6,562.50	$15,312.50
3	50%	$4,375.00	$19,687.50
4	25%	$2,187.00	$21,875.00

Step 6:
Calculate payout
for quarter

Subtract previous
quarter earnings from
cumulative incentive
earned.

Quarter 1 earnings are
$8,750. Quarter 2
earnings are $7,090.
Quarter 3 earnings are
$18,160. Cumulative
earnings are $59,200.
$59,200 − $18,160 −
$7,090 − $8,750 =
$25,200
Quarter 4 payout =
$25,200
Total earnings for year:
$8,750 + $7,090 +
$18,160 + $25,200 =
$59,200

Appendix B
Sales Compensation Surveys

Publishing Company	Survey Title	Web Site
The Alexander Group, Inc.	2001 Annual Sales Compensation Survey: Software Industry	www.alexandergroupinc.com
Aon Consulting/Radford Division	Radford Sales Compensation Survey	www.radford.com
Clark/Bardes Consulting	Sales^{Plus} Survey of Customer Focused Positions	www.clarkbardes.com
Culpepper and Associates, Inc.	CulpepperNOW SalesPay	www.culpepper.com
Hewitt Associates LLC	Sales Compensation Survey	www.hewitt.com
McLagan Partners, Inc.	Sales and Marketing—US	www.mclagan.com
William M. Mercer, Inc.	High-Tech Industry Sales Compensation Survey	www.imercer.com
William M. Mercer, Inc.	Sales Performance and Compensation Survey	www.imercer.com
Organization Resources Counselors, Inc.	Survey of Sales Compensation in the Consumer Products Industry	www.orcinc.com
Organization Resources Counselors, Inc.	Survey of Sales Compensation in the Medical Devices Industry	www.orcinc.com
The Management Association, Inc.	2000–2001 National Sales Compensation & Practices Survey	www.mranet.org
Thobe Group, Inc.	Communication Technologies Sales Compensation Survey	www.thobe.com
Top Five Data Services, Inc.	MEDIC (Medical Device Industry Compensation) Sales Compensation Survey	www.top5.com
Watson Wyatt Data Services	ECS Survey of Sales and Marketing Personnel Compensation	www.ecssurveys.com
Western Management Group	High Technology Sales Compensation Survey	www.wmgnet.com

Appendix C
Software Vendors—
Sales Compensation
Administration Software

Company Name	Web Address
Advanced Information Management, Inc.	www.aimworld.com
The Alexander Group, Inc. (AGI) Software Services	www.alexandergroupinc.com
Callidus Software, Inc.	www.callidussoftware.com
CDS Solutions Group	www.cdsgroup.com
Centive, Inc.	www.centive.com
Convergent Solutions	www.convergents.com
DSPA Software Inc.	www.dspasoftware.com
GlobeNet Technologies	www.globenettech.com
Iconixx Corporation	www.iconixx.com
Jenkon	www.jenkon.com
Motiva, Inc.	www.motiva.com
NetView Technologies, Inc.	www.netviewtechnologies.com
Oracle Corporation	www.oracle.com
PeopleSoft, Inc.	www.peoplesoft.com
SAP	www.sap.com
Siebel Systems, Inc.	www.siebel.com
Stonewater Systems, Inc.	www.stonewatersystems.com
SuperPowerNet.com, Inc.	www.superpowernet.com
Synygy, Inc.	www.synygy.com
Taltos Software	www.taltossoftware.com
Trilogy Software, Inc.	www.trilogy.com
ViComp Management, Inc.	www.vicompmgt.com
Vipar Systems, Inc.	www.vipars.com

Index